What People ...
Sean Feucht and Andy Byrd and *Integrity*...

"There are few issues that are as crucial for this generation to understand as the issue of integrity. I am so grateful that my friends Sean Feucht and Andy Byrd gathered key insights from Christian leaders who, from years of experience and biblical insight, invite us on the journey of integrity that draws us closer to God. Understanding this empowers us to change the world. Sean and Andy have not merely written about integrity, but have a passion to walk in it that I have experienced firsthand. In their own lives as leaders, husbands, and fathers, the authors of this book have committed to living a life of integrity that is to be admired and replicated."

—*Banning Liebscher*
Founder and pastor of Jesus Culture

"I love this book! Sean Feucht pulled together a group of leaders that emulate integrity and share not only the 'how to' but the 'why should we' of the character journey. You will find yourself making new choices in your inner journey with God as you soak up each chapter of this must-read book."

—*Shawn Bolz*
Author, *Translating God*
www.bolzministries.com

The timing of this book, *Integrity*, could not be more perfect. Integrity is one of the most needed characteristics of our time; everyone should aspire to live with integrity to the fullest. I'm thankful that Sean and Andy are bringing emphasis to it in this season. I am excited that this book is in your hands as it is a very worthy investment of your time to read—and to become more full of integrity.

—*Eric Johnso*n
Senior leader, Bethel Church, Redding, CA
Author, *Christ in You* and *Momentum*

INTEGRITY

CHARACTER OF THE KINGDOM

SEAN **FEUCHT**

ANDY **BYRD**

CHÉ **AHN**

HEIDI **BAKER**

STACEY **CAMPBELL**

DARLENE **CUNNINGHAM**

DICK **EASTMAN**

JAMES W. **GOLL**

ALLEN **HOOD**

CINDY **JACOBS**

CHARLES **STOCK**

I NTEGRITY

CHARACTER OF THE KINGDOM

FOREWORD BY **BILL JOHNSON**

WHITAKER
HOUSE

Integrity: Character of the Kingdom

Sean Feucht
www.burn24-7.com

ISBN: 978-1-62911-550-4 • eBook ISBN: 978-1-62911-572-6
Printed in the United States of America
© 2016 by Sean Feucht

Whitaker House
1030 Hunt Valley Circle
New Kensington, PA 15068
www.whitakerhouse.com

Library of Congress Cataloging-in-Publication Data
Names: Feucht, Sean, author.
Title: Integrity : character of the kingdom / Sean Feucht and Andy Byrd, Heidi Baker, James W. Goll, Darlene Cunningham, Dick Eastman, Stacey Campbell, Ché Ahn, Cindy Jacobs, Allen Hood, Charles Stock.
Description: New Kensington, PA : Whitaker House, 2016.
Identifiers: LCCN 2015048896 | ISBN 9781629115504 (trade pbk. : alk. paper)
Subjects: LCSH: Integrity—Religious aspects—Christianity.
Classification: LCC BV4647.I55 I58 2016 | DDC 241/.4—dc23 LC record available at http://lccn.loc.gov/2015048896

2 3 4 5 6 7 8 9 10 11 12 **UJ** 23 22 21 20 19 18 17 16

CONTENTS

FOREWORD

BILL JOHNSON

It has always been a passion of mine to study and learn from those who have a strong heritage of faith—to be instructed by the godly legacy left behind by men and women of God. Too many of us are sure that we're doing everything right, that we have it all under control, until we compare our steps with those wise ones who have been walking with the Spirit for years. Then we may notice that our steps are looking a little shaky!

The extraordinary array of authors in this book, many of whom I know personally, are examples of such wise men and women of God. And their insights recorded here are especially compelling because they are intensely honest. Heidi Baker, James Goll, Darlene Cunningham, Dick Eastman, Stacey Campbell, Ché Ahn, Cindy Jacobs, Allen Hood, and Charlie Stock will take their place in history as heroes of the faith—but they're not afraid to get real. They're not afraid to tell the truth about God, about their lives, about our daily battle with darkness.

And that's what the millennial generation needs.

I know that this generation is filled with a fervency for service—I've seen these future leaders outdoing themselves in my church's Bethel School of Supernatural Ministry. But I also know that these young people need more than action: they need character. They need more than fine words; they are craving examples of Christ-followers who are unafraid to tell the truth. They need more than moments of intense emotion; they are longing for consistent, day-by-day rootedness in their foundation, Christ. They need this book!

I've been in ministry for years, and I've seen how easy it is for people to hide the truth, to be obsessed with appearances, and to live under a disguise. How many of us are saying one thing and living another? Being vulnerable and honest is never a popular step, but it is a vital step forward in the kingdom of God. I think Sean Feucht and Andy Byrd shot a bulls-eye when they prophesied the need for a movement of integrity. I've witnessed the need all over the world in the faces of people who are eager to live like the Man who said, "I am the truth."

In *Integrity: Character of the Kingdom* you have an incredible, precious compilation of original thoughts from people who have walked the road you're trying to walk and are now showing you the way. I was encouraged and challenged to discover how these voices, although all gathered separately, join together to utter in similar tones one refreshing message: Live in truth, in every aspect of life, through every difficulty, despite what anyone thinks. Live in truth. That's the harmonious message of this choir of prophets and saints.

I only wish I'd had a book like this years ago!

ONE

SEAN FEUCHT AND ANDY BYRD

Integrity: A Loving Response to the Holiness of God

Sean Feucht is a husband, father, missionary, musician, speaker, author and founder of a grassroots global worship, prayer, and missions organization: Burn 24/7. His lifelong quest and dream is to witness a generation of burning hearts arise across the world with faith, vision, and sacrificial pursuit *after the presence of God. He travels to twenty to thirty nations per year, training, mobilizing, leading worship, speaking, and planting furnaces of worship and prayer. He has produced, recorded, and released fifteen music albums, numerous books, and teaching resources. When not on the road, he lives in Harrisburg, Pennsylvania, and is obsessed with his wife, Kate, and their three children.*

Andy Byrd and his wife, Holly, have dedicated their lives to spiritual awakening in a generation. Andy is part of the leadership of University of the Nations, YWAM Kona and has been with YWAM for fifteen years traveling to many different nations with a heart to raise up a revival generation to live in the confluence of a zealous love for God and a sincere love for others! Andy and Holly have helped give birth to Fire and Fragrance ministries and the School of the Circuit Rider. They have five children.

Sean and Andy have had the honor of running together in deep friendship for the last eight years. Out of their friendship, they have had the chance to impact many lives, travel to many nations, ignite missions and prayer initiatives, and coauthor several books. This book came out of a shared desire to live their lives in a way that would make integrity famous in a generation. Their hope is that a whole generation will rise up with a zeal to live in an integrity that pleases God and changes the world.

Integrity! A loving response to the holiness of God! A joy-filled heart motivation to live true to the revealed character of our all-sufficient, all-perfect, all-loving God!

We can't make it up, fake it, or contrive it. That is not integrity. We either have it or we don't. Integrity begins in the heart and mind as a godly motivation behind our words, thoughts, and actions. From this place of inward purity and selflessness comes action that will reflect the integrity of our hearts. These actions are as discernable as white paint on a black wall in our society where greed, dishonesty, manipulation, and immorality run rampant. Those that walk in integrity truly are a light in the world. They may be a rare light on a landscape dominated by the dark, but anyone who has seen a lighthouse from the ocean at night or seen a distant city from far away knows the power that a single light can bring. Over two thousand years ago, a single light was sent from heaven that lit a remote corner of Bethlehem, a single light so bright that the whole world would soon be impacted. Two thousand years later, that light has spread to billions.

Unfortunately, as many have realized, that light of Christ is not bursting out of the church like it should be. It is as if our light is at times dim, filtered, and sometimes even snuffed out. We will only reclaim the brilliant light of Christ if we, as a whole body, embrace integrity!

LET'S MAKE INTEGRITY FAMOUS IN A GENERATION

The need could not be more immediate or more real. So many have lost their moral compass. The very definition of what is true, good, righteous, and holy is under violent assault. A generation is growing up with the wrong values touted at home, in school, and in the media. The perfect body, the biggest bank account, and the most power are promoted as the highest aims in life. Politics is full of blatant criticism between factions and one scandal after another in the personal lives of politicians. Honesty is rarely even mentioned. Our education system has replaced the revealed truth of Scripture with fabricated attempts to explain away God's existence.

Where is integrity in the marketplace? Another CEO stealing money, another report of sweatshops and child labor, another fraudulent business scheme. There has been a steady regression from an ethic of hard work, provision for our families, honesty, and uprightness to an ethic of putting self first, worshipping money, and cutting as many corners as possible without getting caught.

Where is integrity in the "heroes" of our day? All we can see is another celebrity in a broken marriage, having multiple affairs, and promoting drugs, sex, abuse, and a lifestyle of self-centered pleasure. Some of the greatest athletes conduct lifestyles just as decrepit as their muscles are toned. They live unreflectively through decades of deception.

Unfortunately, the church has not always outshone the world in areas of integrity. Whether it be a leader falling into a financial or sexual scandal or a man straight out of Sunday church, still dressed up in suit and tie, rudely chewing out the waitress who got his order wrong, we often live hypocritically instead of *Him-focusedly*. Does the world look at the church and see the integrity of Christ? Does the world look at Christians and see a different way of thinking and living? Or do Christians just melt right into the systems around us, falling into the same addictions, the same dishonesty, the same immorality, and the same me-centered living? A torrent of lies originating from a very real enemy that hates all of God's created sons and daughters form a raging river seeking to sweep the lost and saved together into a sea of selfishness that leads only to death.

But...

It is not too late! It never has been too late. This is not the first time we have looked around at a sin-soaked world and thought, *Things should be different!* We have been here before, and many times it is in the valley where the light begins to grow! It starts with just a few who persist despite the shadow of death. A David on the back hills of Bethlehem, or a Daniel enslaved with three friends in the courts of a Babylonian king, or a Samuel miraculously born and then given up by his mother to be raised in the presence of God by a priest. Each time there was a dark valley...

each time there was a small light...each time there was a great turning back to God's heart!

It is not too late because of *you*. Because you picked up a book on integrity when so few are even talking about this topic. All the world needs is a "you" whose heart is alive with Christ, whose mind is in love with truth, whose actions are a stream of joyful obedience to the One we adore! You are the hope in a world where the blind are leading the blind! You are not blind! We were blind, it's true... but now we see. We were dishonest, greedy, and selfish...but now we are filled with the love of Christ, and He rules and reigns where "self" used to! We have a new Man on the throne and that Man's blood and body and conquering of death opened the doors for a grace to fall on every one of us! We can now walk in fierce determination to do what is right and pleasing to Him.

It is not too late because we have an example. Because we have real heroes to follow, real heroes who exercise integrity. We, Sean and Andy, would be the first to say that we only want to learn more about how biblical integrity is actually walked out. We are eternally grateful for grandparents and parents who modeled integrity in amazing ways. We have seen integrity, we have experienced integrity, but in no way would we consider ourselves qualified to write a book calling an entire generation to integrity. Rather, we join the sea of faces that are eagerly looking to our mothers and fathers, who have lived, modeled, and at times failed at but still persisted in, integrity. They stand as pillars in the house of God of what integrity looks like. We asked nine heroes of integrity to share their knowledge and experience. There is no greater collection of fathers and mothers I could present before you as the model of God's dream. They have all encountered extravagant loss, hardship, temptation, and at times insurmountable pressure to give up and compromise. Yet, they have all prevailed and stood strong. So, with great anticipation we look to the pages that fill this book from true moms and dads who have shown us the way!

WHAT IS INTEGRITY?

As we look ahead to the pages in this book and chapters on specific areas of integrity, let's get a simple definition in our minds of what integrity *is* and outline a few things that it is *not*.

According to the dictionary, "integrity" is the adherence to moral and ethical principles; soundness of moral character; honesty. It is also defined as the state of being whole, entire, or undiminished.[1]

The Bible refers to integrity many times, sometimes using the exact word "integrity" and other times describing attributes of a life and character of integrity.

> *Better is a poor man who walks in his integrity than a rich man who is crooked in his ways.*　(Proverbs 28:6 ESV)

> *The integrity of the upright guides them, but the crookedness of the treacherous destroys them.*　(Proverbs 11:3 ESV)

> *Finally, brothers, whatever is true, whatever is honorable, whatever is just, whatever is pure, whatever is lovely, whatever is commendable, if there is any excellence, if there is anything worthy of praise, think about these things.*
>
> (Philippians 4:8 ESV)

Integrity is not perfection, nor should it even be confused with character. It is an aspect of character. But one can have integrity even while one is yet on the journey to a more godly character, because integrity starts at a heart, a mind, and a primarily motivational level. It is the unwavering determination to do what is right. Someone might still be struggling to walk that integrity out in all areas of character, in thought, word, and action. But God sees the

---

1. "Integrity," http://dictionary.reference.com/browse/integrity (accessed December 30, 2014).

motivation of the heart and sees the fierce desire to overcome, to walk in truth and love-based action!

It must also be said that integrity void of love is no longer integrity. If integrity is defined as being upright, whole, and adhering to moral and ethical principles, then we must recognize that love is the highest ethic we have been called to as believers: love for God, love for each other, and love for the lost. To try and have integrity without love is to build a tower of unimpeachable morality where we live isolated from reality and the needs of people around us. The outside world feels the coldness and distance of this type of integrity. Rather, think of integrity as the banks of a river that is flowing throughout the land, offering living water everywhere it goes. The river's impact is massive and it is constantly inviting us to come and experience abundant life. Yet it is kept within its God-ordained parameters by the riverbanks, which keep it from destructive overflow. Those strong riverbanks are the integrity of our lives, and the river is the love that is accessible and inviting to all. Our integrity should be irresistibly attractive to the broken, the lost, and the hungry in heart. Love is that attractive force in our integrity. Without love, it ceases to be integrity!

As I (Andy) was writing my part of this chapter, I was also painting the deck on my house. There are two ways to paint any exterior surface. One way is to paint it just so that it looks good. The other way is to paint it so that it not only looks great, but so that the wood is actually protected from the elements. The temptation is to quickly slather color only on the wood that can be seen—ignoring underneath the deck or the part that's hidden by the massive juniper bush. However, only wood that has been painted on all sides will stand the test of time against sun and rain.

Far too many people want to have just enough character to seem godly to their neighbors and friends. They colorfully paint whatever part of their life is visible, and ignore the invisible parts. That is not integrity; that is not character. That is hypocrisy.

And that could be part of the very problem that's breaking down our society. A life of integrity is a life that is painted on all sides with godliness—the sides that people see and the sides that they don't—and a life that is therefore protected from the temptations and lies that will constantly assail us.

THE PROMISES THAT PROPEL US

However severely we are gripped by the dire crisis of the integrity-less nature pervading the body of Christ, fear alone will not be the mechanism that brings lasting change. Reactionary living does not motivate and rarely ever sustains. In fact, many times a response in fear motivates us to become the very thing we hate.

Scientific studies continually reveal that the results stemming from positive motivation are far more beneficial than those from fear of negative consequences. A recent Harvard University School of business study, for example, tracked, studied, and interviewed fifty thousand individual business leaders to determine the ideal "praise-to-criticism ratio" for optimal effectiveness.[2] The findings blew away past precedents; the number of needed positive comments was much higher than previously surmised. The most effective and highest performing leaders were receiving almost six positive comments to every one negative (5.6 to 1, to be exact). The modern human psyche is much more apt to change and excel when motivated by encouragement and benefits rather than when motivated by fear and failure.

This statistical information applies to more than just the business world. I have personally found this to be true in marriage, business, life, and my personal walk with the Lord. This approach is a game-changer in the way we witness! Isn't it time for the world to know more about the abundant promises that

2. Jack Zenger and Joseph Folkman, "The Ideal Praise-to-Criticism Ratio," *Harvard Business Review*, March 15, 2013, https://hbr.org/2013/03/the-ideal-praise-to-criticism.html (accessed January 6, 2016).

accompany Christ-like character rather than knowing more about the condemnation for rejecting it? Most are already living in some form of condemnation and this has contributed to further depths of depravity. We have no excuse for ignoring the biblical and theological validity to the claim that negative consequences invariably follow a corrupt character. But the over-abundance of benefits and life-altering promises are what actually stir the desire for a higher existence and propel us to greatness. Clearly, the "Jesus way" to launch a cultural revolution in the midst of a broken, wicked, and immoral society is not with fear and condemnation. Instead, His weapons were hope, kindness, and the promise of a better life— the assurance of salvation. *"For God did not send his Son into the world to condemn the world, but in order that the world might be saved through him"* (John 3:17 ESV).

It is His beautiful promise of a better and eternal life that actually woos mankind out from our crooked ways leading to death. In one way, it is really no sacrifice for us to surrender our life of assured death in order to inherit eternal abundance. What a privilege! It is His faithfulness and patience with our hard hearts that draws us closer. It is His kindness that leads us into the ways of godliness and integrity.

The greats of the Bible saw both the short- and long-term rewards of integrity, and it drove them to stay true and steadfast through very difficult circumstances. Although they were all incredibly gifted, called, and anointed, I believe the daily act of beholding these rewards with a heavenly-minded vision is what distinguishes them as pillars of the faith. The apostle Paul's mandate was to *"press on toward the goal for the prize of the upward call of God in Christ Jesus"* (Philippians 3:14 ESV). Peter's drive was to supplement *"faith with virtue"* in order to keep one from being *"ineffective or unfruitful in the knowledge of our Lord Jesus Christ"* (2 Peter 1:5, 8 ESV). These two apostles were not passive, lethargic, or indifferent in their pursuit of integrity and truth, and the longstanding fruit of their lives shows it. Let us learn from their resolute discipline and surpassing joy!

To whet your appetite for the teaching, testimonies, and personal experiences in this book from contemporary heroes of the faith, let us explore a few of the many biblical promises afforded to those who live a life of integrity. This is by no means an exhaustive list, but the few discussed here are highlighted again in the following chapters.

BECOMING THE DREAM

It has become fairly normal and almost celebrated to become the naysayer, cynic, and finger-pointer of all that is wrong with the church and society. Entire books, movements, and cultures are built around fragmenting the church and pointing out her every flaw. These people, institutions, and societies are known more for what they stand against than what they actually stand for. Many in this camp feel they are the ultimate "policeman" who is entitled to explain how things should be run more responsibly, more efficiently, and more virtuously.

This is not who we are or what this book is about. This book is about a godly lifestyle, as famous preacher Chuck Swindoll explained in his devotional *Day by Day*, "Few things are more infectious than a godly lifestyle. The people you rub shoulders with every day need that kind of challenge. Not prudish. Not preachy. Just spot-on clean living. Honest-to-goodness, bone-deep, non-hypocritical integrity. Authentic obedience to God."[3]

The road to possess integrity begins and ends with humility and the recognition that we all have room to grow, change, and increase in godly character. The plank in our own eye must be acknowledged and removed before we can hope to "*stir up one*

---

3. Chuck Swindoll, "The Art of Persuasion," Oneplace, www.oneplace.com/ministries/insight-for-living/read/devotionals/todays-insight-from-chuck-swindoll/day-by-day-august-10-2011-11654724.html.

another to love and good works" (Hebrews 10:24 ESV). Not only do our remarks of criticism appear hypocritical to the world, but they are offensive in the eyes of Jesus. After all, He gave His very life for the church we so casually bash. As we pursue integrity together, we must cast off the grumbling, do away with the finger-pointing, and fully step into becoming the dream of God for a generation. When we fully embody and model His dream, it gives us authority and attraction to transfer what we carry to everyone we know. If we want to shine, we must live blamelessly.

> *Do all things without grumbling or disputing, that you may be blameless and innocent, children of God without blemish in the midst of a crooked and twisted generation, among whom you shine as lights in the world.* (Philippians 2:14–15 ESV)

Let's discover three distinct and guaranteed promises for the life of integrity clearly laid out in the Scriptures below.

Promise #1: The reward of His presence

> *Because of my integrity you uphold me and set me in your presence forever.* (Psalm 41:12 NIV)

These very words ignited a fire inside my (Sean's) heart. I'll never forget the day this promise completely blindsided me and set my heart on a journey to pursue the cause of integrity with crazy passion! For days, weeks, and months, I meditated on this concept so beautifully penned by the psalmist. It convicted my heart while consuming my thoughts and desires! My spirit was provoked to journey with the Lord for a breakthrough of integrity in my own heart. This does not mean I did not believe it was important before, but something in this promise broke off any passivity and set me on a tenacious course to grab hold of it.

The way we worship has dramatically changed in the last thirty years, shaped largely by theology and teaching that encourages every seeking heart to experience God's nearness, and I have benefited hugely from that change. In many ways, we have progressed from understanding the Holy Spirit with our minds to experiencing Him in our hearts and emotions. He is the God who is readily available, accessible, and actually searching *"to and fro throughout the whole earth, to show Himself..."* (2 Chronicles 16:9). The current "presence-seeking" generation has shrugged off the yoke of religion and performance to delve into experiencing the fullness of God's delight. This is our lone pursuit and our great reward as the children of God.

I and other believers with me experienced this hunger for God's presence, and it spurred a roomful of ragtag musicians to worship through the night in my dorm room eight years ago in Oklahoma. I will never forget hitting those "sweet spots" in the middle of the night when it seemed all of heaven crashed into the room. Often it was after far too much coffee had been consumed, and we had run out of songs to sing or prayers to pray. We just waited and gazed in complete weakness, surrender, and dependency for Him to show up. There was absolutely no plan nor drive to launch a worldwide ministry. Nevertheless, a movement was born that day. It was His presence alone that motivated our pursuit.

Yet the dynamic truth behind this verse from Psalm 41 declares that passion and hunger are not enough to sustain this "presence-centered" life style. All-night prayer meetings, emotional worship, and a rage of unrelenting passion can surely signify His presence. But something far more costly and sustainable is required to keep us in the "sweet spot" of God's nearness: integrity. We need a great reformation in our lives and communities to provoke the longing to live rightly before God.

God is looking for *"truth in the inward being"* (Psalm 51:6 ESV) and a worshipper whose substance is more than momentary passionate prayers and the occasional burst of a boisterous song. Although He loves to respond to us out of His mercy and grace in those moments and seasons, it is integrity that "upholds" and "sets us" in His presence forever. It is integrity that sustains His presence and favor in our lives hourly, daily, weekly, and into eternity!

This is not about "earning" His presence or goodness through works, but more about positioning our hearts for the maximum reward of His continual nearness. An increased capacity to feel and experience God's presence is available to those who position their hearts in a posture of godly character. After all, it is the *pure in heart*" who shall see God (Matthew 5:8 ESV). Purity in the sight of God empowers us to see things in God that would otherwise be invisible. The entire calling and purpose of abiding in His presence is to be further transformed, renewed, and empowered to behold all that God has for us.

Let's look at that verse one more time: *"Because of my integrity you uphold me and set me in your presence forever"* (Psalm 41:12 NIV). Oh for a generation to be upheld in the presence of God alone! We find this promise repeatedly throughout Scripture but never so eloquently than in this verse. I believe the focus on "forever" is the most powerful facet of this promise. It speaks of an eternal reward that lasts beyond the music, passion, and reputation—even beyond our earthly lives. This eternal reward far outweighs any earthly blessing of possessing integrity (of which there are many). The life of integrity is the life of one that will echo with rewards into all of eternity.

Promise #2: Promotion that sustains

> *So you will walk in the way of the good and keep to the paths of the righteous. For the upright will inhabit the land, and those with integrity will remain in it.*   (Proverbs 2:20–21 ESV)

Not only does the cultivation of integrity position our hearts to sustain and remain in the presence of God, but it also provides a foundation by which we can receive and succeed in the promises of God. Stewardship is such a big issue in the eyes of the Lord. The resources of the kingdom are aligned in our lives according to what we are able to steward, and if there's a limit to our portion, the reason for it lies within ourselves. Although the dream of God for each of us is *"exceedingly abundantly above all that we ask or think"* (Ephesians 3:20), there is a progression to how these plans and promises manifest in our lives. In 1 Corinthians 10:13, the Lord states that He promises not to place us in situations *"beyond what you can bear"* (NIV).

God is not withholding from us like a cosmic vending machine who won't release your inheritance until you feed it enough good works, but rather like a Father whose vision is far bigger, grander, and more sustainable than ours. The question is not how much will He give, but how much can we bear? How strong and steadfast is the foundation of our character? How resolute is our ability to hold fast to our values in the face of our raging, temptation-filled world? Every promotion in the kingdom brings a greater level of responsibility and an increased pressure. God will not entrust the gift of His greatest dreams to a people who do not have the foundation to steward them. Otherwise the gift alone would destroy us! The taller the tree becomes, the deeper and wider the roots must go to support it. It is the same way in the kingdom of God. The courageous Rosa Parks, who stood strong staring down racial injustice and shifting the course of an entire nation, is supposed to have said, "Stand for something or you will fall for anything. Today's mighty oak is yesterday's nut that held its ground." It is for us to go the distance and finish strong until our very last breath. God's desire for us is to echo, at the end of our days, the words of the apostle Paul: *"I have fought the good fight, I have finished the race, I have kept the faith"* (2 Timothy 4:7).

There is a biblical correlation between adhering to godly principles and an increased capacity to inherit the dreams, plans, and promises of God. The favor of God will open doors of promotion before us, but it is the "rock-like" character we possess that will keep us positioned there. It has been said in revival history: "To a people without mixture, He will give the Spirit without measure." There is no end to the "measure" of God available to the consecrated and upright hearts!

To echo the words of the great American president Thomas Jefferson: "In matters of style, swim with the current; in matters of principle, stand like a rock." How many anointed Christian leaders, businessmen, pastors, actors, musicians, and evangelists carrying an extraordinary measure of favor and gifting have traumatic public failures at the height of their careers and ministries? Whether moral, financial, marital or some other exposed failure, the consequences in their lives, families, and the church were devastating. The examples of this are endless both in our current society and throughout revival history.

We can no longer correlate a dynamic personality, gifting, or apparent favor with a lifestyle of godly character and integrity. Romans 11:29 is very clear that *"God's gifts and his call are irrevocable"* (NIV). Although this issue is alarming to many believers, the truth is that God allows people to be incredibly successful, profitable, and walk in apparent favor without truly possessing a foundation of integrity. Yet a "remaining" in the place of favor is reserved for the *"upright"* and those with *"integrity of heart."* What a paradigm-shifting truth to propel us along this journey of pursuing integrity! The reward of "remaining" in the promotion He brings is truly worth the cost to live a life of godly character.

> Integrity is built by defeating the temptation to be dishonest; humility grows when we refuse to be prideful; and endurance develops every time you reject the temptation to give up.
> —Rick Warren

Promise #3: Establishing legacy

And as for you, if you will walk before me, as David your father walked, with integrity of heart and uprightness, doing

according to all that I have commanded you, and keeping my
statutes and my rules, then I will establish your royal throne
over Israel forever, as I promised David your father, saying,
"You shall not lack a man on the throne of Israel."

(1 Kings 9:4–5 ESV)

The decision to journey for integrity may begin in our hearts, but it has the capacity to carry on into future generations. The sheer opportunity we have for our one small yes of faith in God to reverberate into a multitude of yes's from our future children's children is one of the greatest privileges on the earth. Living for a generation we will never see is a powerful legacy.

God consistently reiterates that He is the God of three generations: Abraham, Isaac, and Jacob. (See Exodus 3:6; Acts 3:13; Matthew 22:32.) This means that He views vision, success, and legacy in three-generation increments. Most young people do not have a life vision beyond the next five years, let alone three generations! But as we see in the invitation to Solomon, the pathway of integrity comes with a promise that God will extend His commitment to establish our family lineage forever. There is that word "forever" again when referencing integrity! *"The righteous who walks in his integrity—blessed are his children after him!.... Even a child makes himself known by his acts, by whether his conduct is pure and upright"* (Proverbs 20:7, 11 ESV).

We are never promised riches, fame, or even worldly success in this life. But we are all extended the opportunity to live godly, holy, and upright lives in the sight of God and men. Making this choice and following this path ensures our mark on generations to come. What a hope for legacy! What an impact every action, word, and deed can have into eternity!

I am not bound to win, but I am bound to be true. I am not bound to succeed, but I am bound to live up to what light I have.   —attributed to Abraham Lincoln

THE PRECEDENT HAS BEEN SET

As a son of the most integrity-filled man I (Sean) have ever known, I have watched how one life of immovable truth, resolute principle, and upright character can impact the next generation. My life will be forever changed and impacted because of my dad. It remains my highest goal to carry even a small measure of the integrity he embodied. Resisting the lure and pressure of a guaranteed lucrative medical career, my father followed the voice of the Lord into full-time missions. This uprooted my family from the grand mountains of the West to the flurry of the crowded East Coast. I was only eleven years old at the time, but my eyes were wide open to the change. I was fully aware of the sacrifices taking place and had an intimate insight into how my father handled praise, criticism, pressure, and promotion.

His obedience to the call of the Lord throughout it all was unshakeable. Despite church and ministry politics, relational conflict, and financial difficulty, I beheld a resilience in the man that had become a rock for our family. The life of integrity always shines its brightest through the darkest nights. It is a beacon of hope to all lost in the sea of difficulty, dissolution, and hopelessness. I watched my father stare down terminal illness amidst the hopeless reports of many cynical doctors and experts. During his last days on earth, his inner anchoring on the faithfulness and goodness of God was a powerful testimony that swept many skeptics into the kingdom of God. I am who I am today because of him.

In the same way, every author bleeding their heart before you on the pages of this book carries their testimony into your life. It was a complete dream to collaborate and present their examples and convictions on godly character. Knowing all of them personally for many years, I cannot say enough to honor the precedent they have courageously pioneered. We humbly imitate them in pursuing integrity as our highest aim and deepest delight, bearing further testimony to heaven's urgent agenda to provoke young hearts to possess this value in increasing measure. They are heroes of the faith. Who will follow their lead?

Imagine a restoration of the moral compass of a generation. Imagine a whole generation doing business with the integrity of Jesus. Picture marriages with both husband and wife walking in total integrity with one another. Think about whole communities relating to each other in integrity. Dream with us about men who walk in sexual integrity before God and young government leaders who refuse to stoop to anything shifty or shady. Picture a people who love integrity, honor integrity, and who search for it like one would search for diamonds. Imagine what it would look like if every reader of this book became a hero of integrity.

Could we believe together for a revival of integrity in the hearts and minds of multitudes of people? Why not now, why not here, and why not starting with you? Malcom Gladwell, in his book *The Tipping Point*, outlines three components of a viral something that creates a tipping point: the type of message, the type of environment, and the type of people. So let me ask you three questions. What if the message is already in the life of Jesus and the pages of Scripture? What if the current environment of corruption, greed, and selfishness is the perfect environment for a tipping point of integrity? And finally, really think about it: what if you are one of those people?

TWO

HEIDI BAKER

Integrity and Tenacity

Heidi Baker and her husband, Rolland, began Iris Ministries, Inc., now Iris Global, an interdenominational mission, in 1980 and have been missionaries for the past twenty-five years. Heidi was ordained as a minister in 1985 after completing her BA and MA degrees in communications and church leadership at Vanguard University in Southern California. Heidi was powerfully called to the mission field

*when she was sixteen and living on an Indian reservation as
an American Field Service student. She was led to the Lord
by a Navajo preacher. Several months later she was taken up
in a vision for several hours and heard the Lord speak to her
and tell her to be a minister and a missionary to Africa, Asia,
and England. When she returned home to Laguna Beach,
California, she began ministering at every opportunity and
leading short-term mission teams. Rolland and Heidi met at
a small charismatic church in Dana Point and married six
months later after realizing they were united in their calling
and desire to see revival among the poor and forgotten of the
world—a calling that continues in the work of Iris.*

Now faith is confidence in what we hope for and assurance
about what we do not see.   (Hebrews 11:1 NIV)

"GET A BOAT"

On one of our first visits to northern Mozambique, my husband Rolland was piloting our little Cessna bush plane from
Maputo to Cabo Delgado—the province where the Makua people
live. God had already told me to go and get His lost Makua bride,
and I felt strongly that this trip was going to give us a glimpse of
our next season. I asked Rolland to fly us down low, and then
lower—as low as we could go. Rolland laughed and took us down
until we were skimming just over the Zambezi River. We were so
close it seemed I could reach out and touch the crystal blue water.
I leaned over and opened the plane door slightly. I could feel the
spray coming up from the river and misting my arms. It was exhilarating and a little terrifying! Rolland pulled up slightly and we
began to see little villages scattered in between the trees. No roads
connected them. No landing strips. I couldn't see anything around
the village huts at all except for dirt footpaths and some tiny fires.

Suddenly, the spirit of intercession fell on me heavily. I closed the door of the plane and immediately went to the back and lay down on the floor. I start sobbing and weeping—deep, gut-wrenching cries. The Lord was showing me the lost people of those villages. An agonizing feeling, almost like despair, washed over me. I began to pray in tongues. Words boiled up from deep inside my spirit and groanings that cannot be uttered. This was spirit-to-spirit, heart-to-heart prayer. I was crying out for the lost. I said, "God, how are we going to reach these people? There are no roads, there's no runway, they have nothing.... Lord, how are we going to reach them?"

I remember sobbing so much that my eyes swelled shut. "Send me, Lord!" I cried. "Take me, Lord! Send me Lord! I don't care if I give my life for one of those villages, just send me!" And then the Lord very clearly replied, "Get a boat."

I was thrilled. Cabo Delgado is settled along a long, narrow stretch of land by the ocean coast. With a little hiking, we would be able to reach all of those villages by boat. We started with one kayak. Over time we got bigger boats. One was shipwrecked, but the main vessel we use now once belonged to a king of Spain. God has repurposed it to glorify the King of Kings. The former royal suite is now packed with bunk beds for our outreach teams. The upper decks are filled with worship and intercession on each new voyage as we ask God to show us where to go next. We still have wild adventures and many close calls. We've had to be rescued from desperate circumstances by fishermen in canoes more than once, but we love it all. Always remember that even if there is no road, God can give you a boat.

But back to my story: when we landed at the end of that first scouting flight in Cabo Delgado, my heart was on fire for God's Makua bride. I couldn't wait to begin gathering them. Immediately I started preaching on the nearest street corner to the youth selling beads and crafts. I led twelve people to the Lord that first day:

Ishmael, Mohammed, Omar, Ramadan, Saide, another Ishmael, and six others. I think at first they only paid attention because they wanted to sell me things, but they also listened. That listening changed their lives. Some of them are leaders in our ministry now—still passionate lovers of God.

"DON'T BE IN A HURRY"

We moved there in 2002. The promises God places in our hearts are not birthed in one day. I strongly feel the Lord saying, *Don't be in a hurry*. We so often want to be in a hurry, and usually we think we have good reasons. We may want to become fluent in a new language as fast as possible, for example—but the true value of the process is often in sitting with someone and letting them teach us as we become friends. We may want to get a new church built as soon as we can, but doing the work of building together in love is much more important than having the new building.

There are seasons when we are so worried about where we are supposed to go. We can be confused, wondering if God is calling us to the brothel or to the Ivy Leagues. One student in our Harvest School of Ministry was so laid down before the Lord that he was completely willing to go to the poorest of the poor, yet I kept seeing him on Wall Street among the rich and the brilliant, a mover and shaker among the financial elites. I didn't know his background at the time, but later I found out that he was a straight-A student at MIT, one of the best universities in America. As he was lying in the dirt and crying out, "I'll go to the poor, I'll go to the poor!" I felt that the Lord meant to send him to some of the poorest people on the planet—the ones on Wall Street. God was going to send him to the poor who are in disguise. I believe that God is taking each of us into a place of such abandonment that we will say these words with complete sincerity: "Where You go, I'll go. What You say, I'll say. What You pray, I'll pray." All we have to know beforehand is that we are called to love God and to love our neighbors. Love covers everything. God wants to undo you with so much love that you can't help but ooze Jesus. No matter how difficult your calling is, it will be possible for you when you overflow with Him. Love is what enables you to overcome the ups and downs of life. Love— the *action*, not the *feeling*—is to be one with God, because God is Love. (See 1 John 4:8.) Only with love will you be able to live out your life full of integrity, free of shame, faithful not just in the big meetings in front of hundreds, but also in small conversations with a mama in the village or your next-door neighbor. Love comes from intimacy, letting God your Father pour His unconditional love on you.

The other day I was sitting in the village. Even eleven years later, every week when I'm home I'm still in the village on Monday, Thursday, and Friday. Why? It's important to me to keep it real. If I just had to do administration or fundraising, I would not make it a month. If I just had to do "leadership," I would never, ever make it at all. I need to be able to express what God put in me in a way that is very concrete. I can't just talk about it or teach it. I have to live it. Most people never see me there. They don't know exactly what I'm doing. But out there in a hut made of mud and reeds, talking to one or another of my old Makua friends, the way is always low and slow. People sometimes get absolutely exhausted by my process because I'm so slow—but what the Lord gave me to model is just being low and slow enough to stop for the one person He puts in front of me.

BE TENACIOUS

Every time I go to the village or even walk across our center, I ask the children I meet what their dreams are. When we first moved to the northern province, virtually all the communities were filled with hopelessness. They were desperately poor. As we were making plans to open our first school we saw many children walking around with their heads tilted down, pushing their little toes through the dirt with bloated bellies peeking out of ripped t-shirts. A lot of them had discolored hair or skin from malnutrition. They really couldn't think of a dream; they could only think of their next meal. Life here can be such a day-to-day struggle, filled with moment-to-moment problems. Houses are bamboo poles tied together with rubber cord sealed with rocks. The mud walls are covered by grass roofs. Once in a while, someone prospers and has a tin roof. Each rainy season, walls cave in, belongings are ruined, and roofs crash down. After sharing the good news of salvation through Jesus, we are trying to teach communities about baking bricks, making stronger homes that will last, and planning for a happy future. We are asking God for strategies and sustainable solutions. And our people are beginning to dream bigger and bigger dreams. The children take pride in their school uniforms; they are fed at breakfast and lunch, and I hear them telling me they want to be pilots, school teachers, doctors, nurses, and presidents.

Truly, we should expect God to give us great dreams. Some of them will be so far beyond our natural capacity that they seem impossible. One day a few years ago I was swimming in the Indian Ocean off of Pemba. It's one of my very favorite spots to pray. I always feel very free there—no requests, no noise, no distractions. Just clear water and Daddy God holding me in His deep, deep love. As I was gliding along, appreciating the beauty of the sea coral and schools of brilliant fish, I heard the Lord tell me to build a university. It was so clear and sudden that I accidentally sucked water through my snorkel. I spurted my way to the surface. Growing up I had been severely dyslexic. I couldn't spell "mouse" or "horse" or anything. My teachers told me I should look into vocational school because I would never make it to college. Could I start a university?

God had prepared me for this moment, though. When I was sixteen He radically healed me from dyslexia. He told me to go to university, and graduate school, and eventually led me to get my PhD in systematic theology at King's College, University of

London. I pressed through ten years of higher education, my heart burning for the mission field all the while. I longed for nothing more than to preach the gospel among the poor, so I planted a church among the homeless while studying long hours in the library during the day. Often I contemplated dropping out in order move to Africa sooner, but God told me to finish, so I did. When He finally told me to build a university, all those years began to make more sense. I believe He has plans and purposes for each and every one of our lives that will bear glorious fruit if we will simply trust Him.

Tenacity is a vital part of obedience. We have to hold on to our calling no matter what. We rest in Him and He is the ultimate Source of our strength, but we must also persevere when things are hard. Integrity means being honest, whole, and undivided. We want to have integrity before the Lord, being wholly given to Him. We must choose to obey Him even when we don't know why He is asking what He is asking. Our lives are not our own, so we press in to do His will and follow Him wherever He leads, whatever the cost. We look to the One who is worthy, and because He is worthy, we yield; we worship; we love Him.

Some of you need to stop wondering about what is going to happen in the future. It is profoundly important to find time to be in the moment and drink what He is pouring out right now, on this day. It is a tremendous relief when we accept that we do not have to figure everything out before we agree to follow the Lord's voice. We don't always need to know what we are doing. We don't have to be the world's greatest planners; we only have to be sons and daughters. This will become more and more natural to us as we rest in it, because God made us to be His children. He wants us to take a deep breath and drink of Him. When we depend on our Daddy, He is delighted to show us what to do each day. He will show us how to love actively, with integrity, moment-by-moment, even if we don't know the future.

KNOW HIS HEART

One day, I woke up early in the morning with an intense urge to pray for a certain woman in a village who had an infestation of worms. I wanted to bring her food, but at that time I had no idea how to reach her, given all of the other commitments I had. I couldn't go back to sleep. The electricity was off. None of the fans worked. It was sweltering, and the mosquitoes were swarming around me. In the darkness before dawn I called out, "God, I'm trying. I want to feed everyone. I don't want anyone to go to bed hungry." As much as I did want to feed the whole world, though, I also wanted a break. I felt Daddy God speaking His love over me then. I knew that He is the One who will multiply His own love through our lives. He is the One who will feed the people. I felt a great confidence that He would bless the nation's crops specially that year. The Mozambican people had caught His heart, and He would not abandon them. He would be their provision.

We have to know the rhythm of His heart. Sometimes He will call us to press in and push hard, and sometimes He will simply call us to rest. We need to be so connected to Him that we know which moment we are in. We all want to go and reach the world. We all want to bring the lost children home, to carry the tangible glory of God, to see great signs and wonders. We want God to crash in upon our lives. We want to shine with His light. But we cannot simply do this one day a week, at special holidays or at great conferences. We need to stop daily in the secret place. We must set aside time for God to love us and fill us with oil. We can't produce this oil for ourselves. He's the only One who produces what we need. We can't make it, but we can become a vessel. If we won't stop to receive it again and again, we will run spiritually dry and be forced to stop. We will have nothing left to pour out unless we consistently look to Him to replenish us with fresh oil.

To bring back lost children from the streets, you need oil. To minister in a conference, you need oil. To start a university, you need oil. God chooses what He wants to do with me, but no matter what He would have me do, each and every day I want more oil. He is the Potter, and we are the clay. He is the Artist, and we are His brushes. He is the Giver of all good things, and so I am resolved to take the time to be with Him. I will be foolish in the eyes of the wise. I am willing to be undone in front of anyone, in any place. Oh, what can God do with a burning house of glory-love, a lighthouse filled with oil? He can save the lost. He can bring them home to Himself. He can set every captive free. He can heal every sickness. But without oil from Him, we can never be more than a dark and empty house. Focus on His face. Discipline your heart. When your mind wanders, focus on His face. He is beyond worthy of your time, your undivided attention. Remember that "getting stuff done" is not the purpose—rather, *He* is the purpose of all you do. Unless He is your goal, you *will* fall into pride. You will serve yourself, not Him. You will serve your to-do list, not Him. You will serve money—or the lack of it, not Him. To be full of integrity is to serve Him, and Him alone. And when we tenaciously hold on to obedience and walk straight toward Him, He will do incredible things.

I cannot start a university in my own strength, but God can. Over the past eleven years I have been buying land in Mozambique—something my father taught me to do. The first plots for what will become the university campus were bought under a coconut tree for a fraction of what it costs now. We sealed the deal with a simple handshake with a man who had suffered from leprosy. A decade later, the last lot we bought cost $650,000. We've emptied our accounts over and over to invest in this dream of a northern Mozambican university.

Recently Rolland and I were meeting with various Iris Global leaders from around the world. We wanted to hear one another's newest visions for the future and update our collective mission statement. We know that we have a calling to reach the poorest of the poor, and we will certainly go anywhere and do anything to share the love of Jesus, but we also don't want the poor to remain poor. The whole reason we want to reach the most desperate is that we want to see their lives and nations changed with effective strategies from heaven. At that meeting I sat by some of my grown Mozambican sons—men who had grown up living on the streets, begging, stealing, and fighting. One is now the senior administrator of our base, attending law school at night. Another is a pastor in our church and leader of our local media team. I am deeply proud of them, but I still see so many others in such need that it can overwhelm me. There are more than three thousand children in our Pemba school, and almost all of them live in mud huts. They all want a better future. How can we help them all? What does that kind of transformation look like?

Believing for this university has been one of the hardest journeys of my life—but it is also what lights up my world. Everything that can be shaken in our lives has been shaken. Even now Mozambique is tightening its laws concerning foreign workers, severely limiting the number of people who can work or volunteer in the country. We have gone from having sixty full-time missionaries in Pemba to less than twenty as the government rejects visa application after visa application. Even prospective university teachers with doctorates and established track records of starting colleges in other nations are being kept out of the country. A huge struggle remains before us, but we continue to persevere and believe. Jesus is worthy of every sacrifice we make. We are going to train people to shine for Him, and we believe they are going to lead nations. When I return to a place of abiding quietly in His presence, I no longer feel the burden, only faith and joyful anticipation. That is what it means to live in His love! To faithfully listen to His voice, despite everything!

ALL FRUITFULNESS FLOWS FROM INTIMACY

No matter what your dream is, the most important thing in our lives is intimacy with Daddy God because we can do nothing in our own strength. All fruitfulness flows from intimacy. We cannot produce any fruit on our own. Only God can. Two of my most important theme chapters are John 14 and 15.

> *Abide in Me, and I in you. As the branch cannot bear fruit of itself unless it abides in the vine, so neither can you unless you abide in Me. I am the vine; you are the branches; he who abides in me and I in him, he bears much fruit, for apart from Me you can do nothing.* (John 15:4–5 NASB)

We must remain in the vine. It is in this place of rest and worship, where we are simply laid down before the Lord, that we can do all we are called to do. Beloved of God, do not give up! Do not abort your promises. When you are exhausted, when you just want to run away and find some easier and more insignificant job to fill your time, run back to the secret place. Only He can renew your integrity and build your character. Let Him love you. It is so much simpler than we have often thought. It is time to be transformed by His love so that there is no fear in you. Be ruined for everything but His presence. Be utterly abandoned to His love, and nations will be transformed. He is mighty, and nothing is impossible with Him. Stay true to your calling, no matter how high or how low the world views it! What is most important is not being an eloquent speaker, having a healing anointing, or being in any other way a great revivalist. It is simply about being so close to the heart of God that you know what He thinks. Remember that it is Daddy's delight to give you all that His Son won on the cross.

Again, and again: all fruitfulness flows from intimacy. To the degree that we are united with the heart of Jesus, God will bring fruit in our lives. To the degree that we are in love with Him, we will be fruitful. We cannot make revival happen, but we can become so hungry for God that we live as constant bond-slaves of love. We can bow low and incline our ears so that He may pierce them, to mark us as His alone. Then we will run to the darkest places in every corner of this world to proclaim who He is.

"Whatever you did for one of the least of these brothers of mine, you did for me" (Matthew 25:40 NIV). When Jesus said, *"I was thirsty and you gave me something to drink"* (Matthew 25:35 NIV), He certainly referred to the poor and the physically desperate. We drill many wells for them in Africa because they are in very real need of water. But within the mystery of the gospel is also the fact that Jesus refers to those who are simply thirsty for love. In Jesus, God made Himself vulnerable and allowed Himself to feel the very things that we feel on earth. He emptied Himself and came down so that He would feel everything we feel. He knew what it felt like to be hungry, thirsty, and tired, and yet He walked out a perfect life. As we worship Him and serve the ones He loves, we give Him a drink. Just as you eat and drink of Jesus when you truly worship Him, so Jesus wants to be nourished by your worship. When you lay your life down and say to God, "I will go anywhere—where You go I'll go, what You say I'll say, what You pray I'll pray, what You do I'll do!" He is honored and refreshed. Let this be your prayer: whether He sends you to the rich or to the brothels, to ruby mines or suburbs or burning deserts or stadiums, simply be willing to go. Allow Him to send you to the garbage dump or into the government. Anywhere you go, go as His beloved son, His beloved daughter. Stay true to His call.

Let Him draw us into the very depths of His heart. Let Him love you, beloved sons and daughters. He alone is worthy of your whole life. Believe what He speaks over you, and don't worry about whether or not you have the ability to bring His promises about. Tenaciously pursue everything He asks you to do—you only need to take one step at a time. Few callings come to fruition suddenly. All will require tenacity and faith. When everything seems about to fall apart, when sickness or poverty or hardships come, and when people disappoint us, we must press in and seek His face once again. Never lose hope. Live with integrity to your calling.

Some will look at Iris and see only a large ministry, without understanding the thirty-five years of hidden struggle that brought us here. They do not remember the times when we lived on canned pineapples, when our children slept in tents that were alive with rats and bugs, or when we were shot at for no discernible reason. We were willing to do anything to rescue our former orphans from the hell we found them in. We had to be. Life was often very hard. It can be easy to overlook the trials and arduous journeys that others have gone through, but we will all face them in this life. God wants our "yes," our total surrender. He works most through those who are willing to give Him everything they have, even if they do not see the kind of immediate fruit they want.

Fully yielded lovers are the ones who will obey Him day after day, year after year, and decade after decade, remaining faithful even before they see their promises fulfilled. That is the practical definition of integrity. They will tenaciously stay true to their calling even in the waiting, even in the most confusing struggles. They will rest in His love, not in their own strength. I know that God, as the Master Vinedresser, wants to prune and chop away every worry and distraction within us so that He may draw us into the secret place of His heart. The more clearly we understand who we are—sons and daughters of an all-powerful and perfectly loving Daddy—the more fruitfulness we will experience in our lives. We will be able to carry what He has placed in us through any adversity. He will make us fully able to accomplish even the most seemingly impossible of dreams. We cannot focus on our inability. We must gaze, always and forever, into the eyes of the One who is forever able.

THREE

JAMES W. GOLL

"When You Walk Through the Fire": Integrity and Endurance

D r. James W. Goll is the president of Encounters Network, the international director of Prayer Storm, and the founder of God Encounters Training—an eSchool of the Heart. He is a member of the Harvest International Ministries apostolic team and an instructor in the Wagner Leadership Institute.

With great joy, James Goll has shared Jesus in more than fifty nations, teaching and imparting the power of intercession, prophetic ministry, and life in the Spirit. James is the prolific author of numerous books, including The Seer, The Lost Art of Intercession, The Coming Israel Awakening, Deliverance from Darkness, A Radical Faith, *and many others. In the spirit of revival and reformation, James desires to facilitate unity in body of Christ by relational networking among leaders of various streams and backgrounds. James has four children, Justin, GraceAnn, Tyler, and Rachel, and multiple grandchildren; he makes his home in Franklin, Tennessee.*

When you pass through the waters, I will be with you; and through the rivers, they will not overflow you. When you walk through the fire, you will not be scorched, nor will the flame burn you.   (Isaiah 43:2 NASB)

I never thought my life would go in the direction it did for over twelve intense years! The lyrics of the world-renowned hymn "Amazing Grace" fits the last several years of my life very well: "Through many dangers, toils and snares, I have already come."[4]

One thing I have learned in my journey in life and ministry can be summed up in Winston Churchill's famous statement: "Never, never, never, give up!" But before I get into all those details, let me personally share with you some of my early years.

FROM HUMBLE BEGINNINGS

I grew up in a small rural town of less than three hundred people in the middle of the United States in Cowgill, Missouri. I was the youngest of three children and the only son to Wayne and

---

4. John Newton, "Amazing Grace," 1779.

Amanda Goll. My family was poor by economic standards, and we struggled to make ends meet. My parents grew up during the Great Depression and married at the height of WWII. Life was hard, but simple.

On July 3, 1951, my mom was five months pregnant with a little boy but had the misfortune of miscarrying the baby. I am often reminded of the words of my dear praying mom, as she would tenderly recite some of the circumstances that surrounded that dreadful day. She would tell me that after her miscarriage, her constant prayer was, "If You will give me another son, I will dedicate him to Christ's service." Similar to the life of Joseph in the book of Genesis, what the devil meant for evil, God turned into good and shifted that painful day into one of destiny and consecration.

My mother's name was Amanda Elizabeth, which could be interpreted as "grace for consecration." God heard my mom's prayers and I was born one year later to the very day on July 3, 1952. I never knew a time in my life that Jesus Christ was not my best Friend and my constant Companion. I have loved the Lord from the earliest possible age and plan on keeping it exactly that way all the days of my life.

My dad was a diligent worker. Eventually he became the manager and later the owner of his own lumberyard. My sacrificial mom made quilts, worked in her gardens, was active in church and civic life, and later became my dad's bookkeeper. We avidly attended the small rural Methodist church and I was the "church mouse." I was there every time the doors were opened. I loved God and I loved singing. I wanted to make a difference in this life.

MY OWN TIME OF CONSECRATION

Being a rather sheltered young man from Missouri, at the ripe age of nineteen-going-on-twenty with big goals of becoming a NASA research biologist, I attended Campus Crusade's Explo '72 at the Cotton Bowl in Dallas, Texas, in June of 1972. Under the convicting preaching of Billy Graham, I stood to my feet with great zeal and total abandonment to dedicate my life to full-time Christian service.

My goal of working for NASA was now on the altar of God. My mother's prayers had prevailed. I surrendered all! I had no idea what this full-time ministry gig would look like. But I did know that my plans for my life were now over. My life's goals and desires were altered forever. I laid down both my pursuit of scientific research and my musical training and ended up receiving a degree in social work. I just wanted to love God and care for people. You see, when I ran smack dab into these strange "Jesus People" in 1972, I met destiny.

With zeal for the Lord, I went from the traditional evangelical church world to riding with unfeigned zeal the unpredictable waves of the Jesus People Movement, which overlapped with the enlightenment of the gifts of the Holy Spirit as I became immersed in the Charismatic Renewal. Later I crossed another significant bridge and dove into the glories of the Third Wave as it crashed upon the shores of church history.

Ultimately I was thrust forth as a regional, national, and then international voice in both the global prayer and prophetic movements, and consultant within the New Apostolic Reformation. What a trip indeed for a skinny kid from a town named Cowgill whose dad only received a sixth grade education.

I went from being an insecure country boy, wet behind the ears, to standing on the peaks of the mountaintops of global exposure and having the honor of impacting leaders of various spheres of society and international influence for Jesus Christ's sake. I served in campus ministry, church planting, and mission endeavors, going from consulting leaders to being a part of various new global networks. I was given a call from the Lord to minister from the "least of these to the greatest of these" among the nations. Like John Wesley, a spiritual guide by Methodist heritage, the world was now my parish.

By His empowering grace, as the years have raced by, I have ministered in well over fifty nations, spoken before hundreds of thousands of people, and written over fifty books and study guides that are translated into multiple languages across the globe. Mountaintops are exhilarating indeed.

WALKING IN TIMES OF UTTER DARKNESS

But peaks are only peaks if they are preceded by, and at times followed by, valleys. Valleys…they are an interesting subject to consider, or better yet, walk through! Psalm 23:4 describes it this way, *"Though I walk through the valley of the shadow of death, I fear no evil, for You are with me"* (Psalm 23:4 NASB). It doesn't say, *"if I walk"* it says, *"though* [or when] *I walk."* For every mountaintop there is a valley. If you want to live a life of integrity, get ready for the valleys.

There is no piercing, penetrating light without the backdrop of darkness. You don't see the stars in the sky in bright daylight. They are still there—but you just don't see them. They only visibly shine forth with brilliant sparkling essence at the darkest midnight hour.

I have tasted life from both sides now as it is described in Romans 11:22, *"Behold then the kindness and severity of God"* (NASB). I have tasted both international acclaim and international controversy. I have gone from perfect health to utter physical weakness. I have gone from a yearly growth in ministry funds to a sudden loss of all my various income streams overnight—from always paying every bill on time to having over $300,000 in debt in foreboding medical bills. I went from having the "Midas touch" to feeling like a beggar.

HOW SHOULD WE THEN LIVE?

The late esteemed theologian Francis Schaeffer appropriately asked the question in his famous book of the same name, "How should we then live?" How do you handle what the desert fathers and Christian mystics called the "dark night of the soul"? What do you do when you experience what feels like not the kindness, but rather the extreme severity of God?

As a Bible-quoting evangelical and then a praying-in-the-Spirit, prophesying charismatic with a name that was internationally known, I still did not have a read for what I was about to encounter—let alone the wisdom for how to endure through it.

Endurance. Sticking it out. Commitment. "Though none go with me, still I will follow. No turning back. No turning back."[5] This endurance piece of integrity is often a missing commodity in the contemporary feel-good culture of the body of Christ today. Hmm. We seem to believe that, if we're going through a valley, then our understanding of God must be wrong. We think, *A good God wouldn't let this happen, would He?* Well, I have searched my heart a thousand times and I can confidently say that I have not lowered the bar of my understanding of God and the Scripture just because my life's experience has not always lined up with the light the Word of God reveals. I still believe God is good; I still believe His Word. But standing in between my life and the Word is like being the taffy in your family's holiday taffy pull, or being the wishbone getting yanked in two directions at once. I was being stretched by opposite tensions, wondering if I was the one who was going to break.

You and I must heed the warnings of Jesus and keep our hand on the plow and not look back, not live life in the rearview mirror. Don't imagine what you think the Lord should have done instead of what He did do. "If only" thinking will destroy you. You see, we need a good dose of raw obedience mingled with the fear of the

5. Anonymous, "I Have Decided to Follow Jesus," nineteenth century.

Lord and an additional unpopular ingredient called old-fashioned perseverance.

How do I keep my hand on the plow (see Luke 9:62) and not look back when things get tough? I have heard this stated scores of times: when the going gets tough, the tough get going. But I'm not sure it's totally accurate. How then shall I live? I think I read in this problem-solving, authoritative book called the Bible that His strength is perfected in weakness. (See 2 Corinthians 12:9.) When I am weak, He is strong. Yes, Jesus loves me. But being full of integrity sometimes means being full of weakness.

The more complex things appear, the simpler my approach becomes. I keep the eyes of my heart focused on the One. I do not veer away from the fear of the Lord. Yet, sometimes He still causes me to tremble, tremble, tremble....

LONG DARK NIGHTS TURNED INTO LONG DARK YEARS

I walked through the valley of the shadow of death with the loss of the love of my life, my dear wife, Michal Ann Goll, in the fall of September 2008. I had the joy and delight of holding this dear woman in my arms for over thirty-two years. We were not just young lovers; we became best friends, parents of four wonderful children, and partners in the Lord's vineyard together. Part of me, at times, still feels like I am missing in action. But life sometimes rudely moves on, and all we can do is persevere.

There are days or even seasons that indelibly mark your life with pain or hardship. How do you respond? How do you hang onto the God of promises when your perception of the promises of God seem to slip away or even evaporate? How do you live with a strong character and integrity even while walking through the valley of the shadow of death?

That disruptive day in 2008 has left a mark on my dear family. Michal Ann was an authentic, modern-day embodiment of incarnational Christianity. She was a role model of what a godly wife, mother, and woman on the frontlines was to be and act like. Loving well was always her aim. But after four hard years of battling colon cancer, after the removal of six organs, after Scripture proclamation, after prayer from gifted healing evangelists mixed with every form of alternative, holistic, and nutritional treatment, she slipped away through the thin veil into eternity. Today she worships nonstop in the authentic 24/7/365. She finished well.

To top it off, while Michal Ann was battling cancer, I endured eight-plus years of non-Hodgkin's lymphoma cancer in three different bouts. I would beat it and it would come back. When I was running on fumes after Ann's death, being a single parent to four kids, attempting to hold together a fragmented family and keep a struggling worldwide ministry afloat, a cancerous tumor the size of a baked potato came raging back behind my stomach.

I learned something simple and ever so dear. I often go back to the solidity of the old hymns for strength and solace. What I learned was this: "I need Him, Oh I need Him; every hour I need Him! O bless me now my Savior, I come to You!"[6] Yes, years later, I am still leaning on the everlasting arms! "What a fellowship, what a joy divine, I'm leaning on the everlasting arms."[7]

Wow, what an unexpected, fiery trial I have walked through these past twelve or so years! There is much more to the trauma that surrounded me, but I think this sampling is enough exposure for you to taste a little bit of what I experienced. It led to questioning, pondering, uncertainty, searching, praying, seeking counsel, resting, trusting, and eventually believing again. Yes, believing that *"God causes all things to work together for good to those who love God, to those who are called according to His purpose"* (Romans 8:28 NASB). That includes me and that includes you.

6. Annie S. Hawks, "I Need Thee Every Hour," 1872.
7. Elisha A. Hoffman, "Leaning on the Everlasting Arms," 1887.

I did not say God caused everything. I did not say everything was good. But I will forever declare that in the mystery and majesty of God and God alone, He can take all our broken, fragmented pieces of life and, if we give them to Him, mess with, mold, and refashion them into something stunning in His sight.

SO, DO YOU HAVE A SPECIAL KEY?

A lot of people know part of my story and ask me if I have a special key that enables me to carry on despite everything that's happened. I don't. Not really. Nothing really distinctly special. Nothing that is not obtainable by the everyday Joe—which, in one manner of speaking, is a description that we all fit into.

Here's my key, if it can be called that: I have never stopped worshipping God. I have never stopped running to Him with my pain. I have never stopped forgiving. I have never stopped seeking counsel and input from the body of Christ. I have never stopped attending church. I have never stopped reading my Bible. I have never stopped praying. I have never stopped believing in miracles. I have never stopped loving God. I have never quit. Quitting is not an option on my list!

But I have wanted to quit many, many times.

I haven't quit, but I have pushed the pause button multiple times to re-evaluate, calculate, postulate, and realign myself. One of my married, adult kids came to me recently and asked, "Dad, you know one of the things I love about you the most?" I did not have a clue what was about to come to next.

"You never stop learning and growing."

WHAT LESSONS CAN YOU PASS ON?

Please realize that I am yet a work in progress. I am still leaning in upon my beloved Jesus and learning a lot these days. But I would be glad to share with you some basic practical concepts that have been anchors in my life along the way and will hopefully lead you to a life of integrity, as well. So here we go with some practical accessible lessons that have helped me to persevere, continue in elementary faithfulness, and never, ever give up.

1. God is good all the time!

I put this at the top of the list on purpose. It is number one for sure! I believe and declare loudly, *"The Lord is good to all, and His mercies are over all His works"* (Psalm 145:9 NASB). If you are going to be an overcomer then you must have this foundational truth in place! Everything else is hinged on this one truth. Always remember, Jesus went about doing good and healing all who were oppressed of the devil. (See Acts 10:38.) He is the same yesterday, today, and forever (see Hebrews 13:8), and He is always going about doing good!

2. All things work together for good.

I hang my hat on this belief system! Romans 8:28 uncompromisingly declares, *"God causes all things to work together for good to those who love God, to those who are called according to His purpose"* (NASB). Well, as I mentioned before, that verse is for me and that verse is for you! It does not say that "everything is good" or that "God causes everything." But somehow in the great majesty of who He is, He takes even our failures, temporary disappointments, and messed-up circumstances and when yielded to Him, He reconfigures them to work together for good! That is the Jesus I know.

3. Keep your expectations high.

Just because I have not seen every person get healed does not mean I am going to stop praying for the sick. Just because everyone does not get saved does not mean I am going to stop declaring the good news of the gospel of the kingdom. In times of darkness, do not doubt what has been revealed in the light. Do not lower your theological bar to match temporary setbacks. Press on. Keep your expectations high and on God. Keep on believing!

4. Rely on a trusted community of believers.

I am so grateful for the body of Christ. Some of you have walked with my family and me through our dark night of the soul. I need Him but I also need you. *"And this is the victory that has overcome the world—our faith"* (1 John 5:4 NASB). It does not say "my faith." It says *"our faith."* We need each other. Sometimes we just need Jesus with flesh on. Be a committed part of the community of believers called the church.

5. Be open to change.

Wow! This is probably been one of the hardest lessons for me. I love consistency and stability. But to make it through to the other side you have to be flexible in the hands of the master Potter. You must learn to recalibrate, adjust, and acknowledge that change is good. Change is not your enemy. Be open to new things, new truths, new revelations, new places, and even new connections. To help cut my monthly budget, I had to move out of my ministry center and into a very small set of offices, and now into virtual offices. I did not like it at first—but it has been good! You may just as well get used to it: things are going to change!

6. Fear not!

Renounce fear! Get delivered of it. Get whatever cleansing is needed. What you fear will come upon you. Fear is not your friend. Fear is the opposite of faith. Fear paralyzes you but faith propels you. Doubt your doubts and trust your dreams. Fear not! He is with you, beside you, and in you. *"Greater is He who is in you than he who is in the world"* (1 John 4:4 NASB).

7. Never, never, never give up!

I have a card I always carry in my Bible. On the outside cover it reads, "Never, Never, Never, Never Give Up!" On the inside it says, "I will never, never, never, never quit cheering for you." Those were my dear late wife's last words to me and our four kids. It was her last prophetic statement to the body of Christ. Jesus is our dread Champion! Put your hand to the plow and do not look over your shoulder. (See Luke 9:62.) Keep looking straight ahead. God is not finished with you yet. He who began a good work in you will complete it! (See Philippians 1:6.) Never give up!

8. I am not a victim! I am a victor!

This is huge and you have to graft this point into your soul. Here is the bottom line: I am not a victim! I am a victor. At one of my low points, one of my kids lovingly got in my face and said something like, "Dad, you got to rise above it. Trauma happens in life. But you must not be its victim." So I am here to tell you that I am a victor in Christ Jesus. He always leads you and me into a triumphant processional. *"But thanks be to God, who always leads us in triumph in Christ, and manifests through us the sweet aroma of the knowledge of Him in every place"* (2 Corinthians 2:14 NASB). You are not a victim! You are more than a conqueror in Christ Jesus!

Now remember, I am still a work in progress. But I pray that you can benefit from the lessons I am learning in life's journey of becoming. After all, it really is a great life! I have lived an amazing life and I am ever so grateful that I have been given a second, third, and even a fourth chance. *"Finally, be strong in the Lord and in the strength of His might"* (Ephesians 6:10 NASB). And when you have done all...stand! (See verse 13.)

FOUR

DARLENE CUNNINGHAM
WITH DAWN GAUSLIN

A Prescription for Integrity
in Communication

From an early age, Darlene Cunningham was aware of a distinct calling from God on her life. The course of that call became clarified forever when she met a handsome, single young man with a vision named Loren Cunningham. When

*she married Loren in 1963, she whole-heartedly took up the
role of cofounding the international mission organization,
Youth With A Mission (YWAM), which he had started in
1960. YWAM is an ever-expanding global "family of ministries" comprised of approximately 20,000 full-time staff from
more than 200 countries and a wide variety of denomina-
tions who serve at more than 1,500 YWAM locations in 187
nations. Some five million students, short-term volunteers, and
staff have served with YWAM since its inception. Darlene
is also the international vice-chancellor of the University of
the Nations (UofN), YWAM's global university founded in
1978. Darlene is a "prime mover" in YWAM in the areas
of facilitation of vision and leadership development and is
eagerly sought as a speaker worldwide. Whatever the context,
she constantly points the hearer to God's faithfulness in every
situation, and to His great grace. One of YWAM's eighteen Foundational Values is "communicate with integrity."
Darlene and Loren currently live in Hawaii, where they lead
the University of the Nations Kona Campus. They have two
adult children and three grandchildren.*

I have a very clear "movie" in my mind of the time and place
where God first convicted me about the need for greater integrity
in my communication.

It was 1967. YWAM was seven years old. Up to that point in
our marriage and ministry, Loren and I had done absolutely everything together. We "lived in each other's pockets" and had discovered how well our gifts worked together. Loren was speaking at a
church in Alhambra, California, where, as he always did and now
still does, he called for young people to join a short-term missions
experience like the upcoming outreach to the islands of the South
Pacific kingdom of Tonga.

Loren and I were planning to head to New Zealand the
very next week to communicate about the Tonga outreach

opportunity. But as he was speaking, I had a clear impression from the Lord: "I don't want you to go on this trip with Loren." I was shocked! There was absolutely no natural reason why I would not go—but my sense of God's direction was very specific.

Loren and I talked about it later that day. He said, "I don't know why either, Dar, but I believe that you have heard from God, and you're not to go." So Loren left for New Zealand without me!

In those days, I would sometimes work at night in my profession as a nurse to help bolster our finances. So I thought that's what I'll do—I'll spend this time of separation working as a nurse. But God had other plans.

The first day Loren was gone, I was lying in bed reading about revival. I remember pulling the covers over my head and shouting, "Lord, will revival always be hundreds of years ago and thousands of miles away? Will I never see revival myself?" The Lord answered me immediately, in that still small voice you hear in your spirit, but it made a thunderously loud impression: "You can see revival when I can trust you with truth."

I was surprised and confused. I thought, I must have gotten a message intended for someone else. I carefully explained to God what a high value I placed on being truthful—that's one thing my parents had pounded into me. Then, it was as if God played back a video in my head, where I could see and hear myself speaking. It exposed all the times and places where I had exaggerated and where I was not careful at all with details. By nature, I am a very positive person, and I wanted things to be seen in the best light, without concerning myself too much with total accuracy. It was not my intention to deceive; it just never occurred to me that my exaggeration was actually lying!

God recalled scene after scene of my life for my conviction. For example, I realized that for years, if there were fifteen people present at an event and someone asked me, "How many people were there?" I would likely cheerfully respond, "Twenty-five or thirty!" I always added a dimension that made the circumstances appear better.

Day after day, while Loren was away in New Zealand, God continued with His laser-beam conviction. *"The LORD detests lying lips, but he delights in those who tell the truth"* (Proverbs 12:22 NLT). Jesus is *"the way, the **truth** and the life"* (John 14:6 NLT). I never did work as a nurse during that season!

The Lord also got my attention through a sermon by Watchman Nee that differentiated between service unto the house of the Lord and service unto the Lord Himself.[8] I realized that much of my exaggeration really came about because I was serving "the house of the Lord," wanting to make the ministry of YWAM look good and be credited for great accomplishments, rather than being focused on the Lord Himself.

God wanted to make this a very big deal in my life. I saw how untrustworthy I really was! If I couldn't be trusted with detail, God could never trust me with the big things I was asking Him for, like revival. In the conclusion to the parable in Luke 16:10, Jesus said, *"If you are faithful in little things, you will be faithful in large ones. But if you are dishonest in little things, you won't be honest with greater responsibilities"* (NLT).

The Lord moved on from exposing my exaggeration to exposing other areas of my dishonest communication: times when I had said I would do something, but did not keep my promise; times when I had been unwise, and my words had been negative and hurtful; even times when I spoke according to my suspicions about people and not out of godly discernment. I deeply repented over each and every situation He brought to my remembrance.

---

8. See Watchman Nee, "Ministry to the House or to the Lord," *A Witness and A Testimony,* May 1966.

PRESCRIPTION FOR CHANGE

I am an "action" person; it's part of my disposition, but also a result of my training as a nurse. So as I repented, there was a specific action plan that God assigned me to do, like a daily medical prescription. I began a personal Bible study to discover what God's Word has to say about communication. I was amazed at how many Scriptures give instruction and commentary about how we speak with one another—both the blessing of our positive communication and the damage caused by our negative communication.

I came up with eighty-four Scriptures on communication that have guided my life—and I'm sure that's not an exhaustive list of what the Bible has to say! Here are a few:

> *May the words of my mouth and the meditation of my heart*
> *be pleasing to you, O Lord, my rock and my redeemer.*
> (Psalm 19:14 NLT)

> *Death and life are in the power of the tongue, and those who*
> *love it will eat its fruit.* (Proverbs 18:21 NASB)

> *The heart of the wise instructs his mouth and adds persuasive-*
> *ness to his lips.* (Proverbs 16:23 NASB)

I wrote them all out on 3 x 5 index cards (there were some positive, practical advantages of living "way back then," in a non-digital age!). I divided the cards up like I would if I were assigning medications for someone who is sick. In the morning, I would read and meditate on three Scriptures; at noon, I did the same; and again in the evening, I would read and meditate on three different Scriptures.

In the cabinet where I kept my honey, there was an index card that I would read aloud whenever I opened the cabinet door: "Darlene—Pleasant words are a honeycomb, sweet to the soul and healing to the bones." (See Proverbs 16:24.) Beside my salt shaker there was another index card that read, "Let your conversation be always full of grace, seasoned with salt, so that you may know how to answer everyone." (See Colossians 4:6.)

I like pretty things, so I especially appreciated the Scripture, *"A word fitly spoken is like apples of gold in a setting of silver"* (Proverbs 25:11 ESV). I pictured that continuously, and the Scripture I hung in my home at the time I first started these Bible "prescriptions" for communication is still hanging in my Kona house today.

I'd like to tell you that I do this perfectly now—that no exaggeration or unrighteous response ever passes my lips. That's not true, but I can say that it happens much less frequently than when I first started this meditation on God's standards for communication years ago. It really is very much like taking a medical prescription when you are ill. At the beginning, you take a lot of meds, like I did with my three-times-a-day Scripture doses. As you become stronger, you just take a maintenance dose. But you are creating a habit and a discipline. There are times in my life when the Lord emphasizes the need for me to realign my communication with His guidelines, so I start taking my "prescription" again. But what has permanently developed is that it now comes much more quickly and automatically to see and say that which is truthful and positive. It has become a lifestyle.

FAITHFULNESS TO KEEP YOUR WORD

In Matthew 5:37, Jesus instructs, *"But let your 'Yes' be 'Yes,' and your 'No,' 'No.' For whatever is more than these is from the evil one."* Wow—that's pretty strong!

When you give your word, you need to keep it! Your word should be solid. Be a man or woman of God who keeps your promise! We can tend to be careless and uncommitted in this regard. But if I accept an invitation to speak to twenty-five people and I get an invitation to speak to a thousand somewhere else, I've already given my word, and I need to keep it: I will speak to the twenty-five. If you have committed to be with a friend and you get a better offer, integrity in communication requires that you don't change your mind. And if you do truly need to be released from a commitment due to illness, family obligations, or another legitimate reason, be sure you communicate thoroughly and apologize for any inconvenience your change in plans may cause to the other party.

God is the author of communication, and He always keeps His word. Numbers 23:19 says, *"God is not a man, that He should lie, nor a son of man, that He should repent. Has He said, and will He not do? Or has He spoken, and will He not make it good?"* Aren't you glad that we can trust and know that God will keep His word? He wants us to be a reflection of Himself to others by keeping our word as well.

But this brings up another area: we should not give our word lightly or indiscriminately. One of the things that's helpful to me in keeping my word is maintaining a lifestyle of actively talking with God about what I commit to—checking in with Him continuously. I truly believe that God is good and He wants the very best for each one of us. So if I have asked God about what I'm doing and He has confirmed it, He knows it is best, no matter what other offers come or how costly it is for me to keep my commitment. To paraphrase something J. I. Packer says in his incredible little devotional *Your Father Loves You*, if we try to think things out in God's presence, He absolutely will guide our minds.

Sometimes we are very intentional about asking God for His guidance for major life decisions: *Where should I go to school? What job should I apply for? Whom should I marry?* But God wants to also be intimately involved in our everyday lives in a relational way. Again, it is being faithful in the little things that matters. Asking for God's input in everyday decisions develops our sensitivity to recognize His voice in the big things as well.

BELIEVE THE BEST ABOUT PEOPLE

It is the meditation of the heart and what we think about people that eventually comes out of our mouths. As Luke 6:45 says, "*A good man out of the good treasure of his heart brings forth good; and an evil man out of the evil treasure of his heart brings forth evil. For out of the abundance of the heart his mouth speaks.*"

Whenever I meet someone, I try to walk in humility—believing the best of them, listening with interest, and not making quick judgments. Sometimes we can tend to pick out weaknesses in others and use them to discredit their input, or to make ourselves appear superior. Or we sometimes don't really listen to *their* story, but use it to tell our own story: "Oh, I've had it so much worse!" Many people just need to be valued by being heard. They don't need us to try to solve their problems; they just need a listening ear.

When people meet me, it is my desire that they would know that I have an open heart—no prejudgments and no "hoops" to jump through to gain my support. With every person I meet, I try to choose to be honest and open in the way I view them—no matter their age, gender, appearance, or nationality. I try to receive everyone with both love and faith.

Instead of prejudging by earthly standards, I try to look to find the gifts and callings God has placed within the individuals I meet. Psalm 139:13–14 says, "*You created my inmost being; you knit me together in my mother's womb. I praise you because I am fearfully and wonderfully made; your works are wonderful, I know that full well*" (NIV84). The Scripture also says that God never removes the gifts He placed within us from the time of conception—whether or not people know Him and serve Him with their gifts! (See Romans 11:29.) God has given me faith to help people discover and develop their gifts for kingdom purposes, which, as God beautifully designed, always gives them personal fulfillment and delight.

LISTEN TO PEOPLE...AND TO THE HOLY SPIRIT

Aside from the words we say, we communicate in many other ways. A simple facial expression can convey disbelief and skepticism or acceptance and interest. The position or stance of our bodies conveys much about our openness to the person speaking. Are we sitting on the edge of our chairs, leaning in to capture every word? Or are we leaning back with our arms crossed, creating a communication barrier? Even the way we dress is an important communicator. People can dress in a sexually provocative way that definitely sends a message, or they can underdress in a situation where they should wear nice attire, thus communicating dishonor and disrespect toward the people they are meeting. Everything matters. Everything communicates.

Listen to what others are saying—and conveying by their body language. But in every situation, also listen to the Spirit! I'm not a statistician, but I've heard that most people speak about 125 words per minute, yet we can receive approximately 400 words per minute. So that gives us a space of 275 words every minute to lean into and "listen" to the Holy Spirit!

DEVELOP DISCERNMENT, NOT SUSPICION

I am fairly analytical in the way I'm wired. I always want to know the question behind the question of what's being said. There are positive types of curiosity and question-asking...but unguarded, these quests can also lead to suspicion, gossip, and judgment.

Again, I remember the time and place when God first began to get my attention about this. I was in the kitchen of our three-room unit in the early days, living on the University of the Nations campus in Kona. There was a leadership meeting going on in the living room that I was not a part of, but because everyone present fully trusted me, I could walk in and out of the meeting, serving drinks and snacks. Suddenly, I realized that although I had served everyone, and there was no legitimate need for me to stay in the room, I was delaying my departure because I was curious about one of the leadership issues they were discussing. I was eavesdropping—there's no softer word for it! God called me up short, and warned me that my curiosity could get me in trouble. We only have grace to carry the things we are anointed and appointed by God to hear, whether it is about financial burdens, people's failures, or any other confidential issue. If we're snoopy, we can come under a weight we were never intended to carry.

With God's conviction fresh on my heart, I began to notice that if I overheard part of a conversation or saw someone do something "suspicious," I would begin to analyze what I knew of the situation and come to conclusions and judgments. But often I only saw part of the picture, and I was not the one responsible to deal with it. God spoke to me strongly that my unrighteous curiosity was not a characteristic of a woman of God, and if I persisted in this unhealthy habit, I would lose my spirit-natural way of thinking; my judgments would develop into a critical attitude. If I didn't change my ways, this curiosity (and sometimes suspicion) would cause me to lose godly discernment. That really scared me and I repented deeply. I asked for godly wisdom and discernment from the Holy Spirit, rather than from my overly-analytical, always-curious flesh.

Another thing came from this conviction about not jumping to half-baked conclusions: now, you can trust that if there is a situation where I am called upon to give input, I will always look to find the right individuals—those who have oversight in that category—to speak for themselves. There are always at least two sides to every story, and it's important to know them all. With incomplete information, you can easily come to wrong conclusions, but if the right people who have firsthand knowledge of the situation are drawn in, much time and emotional energy can be saved.

CONSISTENT TRUSTWORTHINESS

When people have true integrity, you can trust them to be consistent and impartial in their communication. They will not say one thing to your face and another thing behind your back. A true friend will be a mirror of truth to you, helping you to see your blind spots. They won't defend your faults, but they also can be trusted not to join in others' criticism of you. Rather, they will seek understanding, and share insights only if the insights will help you to grow. They will be true to you, whether you are there in front of them or not.

Years ago, when Loren and I were leading the Lausanne, Switzerland, campus, we were all very young and relatively inexperienced. One of our trusted young leaders became involved in an area of moral failure. He immediately came to us, acknowledged his sin, and deeply repented. No one expected it, and there was a certain level of shock.

Because this man carried many responsibilities in our ministry, we needed to have a leadership meeting to discuss the best discipleship process for him and how we would cover the leadership roles that he had been carrying. As we were setting up the chairs for the meeting, Loren put out one too many chairs. I mentioned to him that there were six chairs, and we only needed five. Loren replied, "No, this is the right number." When the meeting started, we all sat in a circle, with one empty chair remaining. Loren started the meeting by saying, "We have to talk about something very difficult tonight, but we will do it with integrity, as though our brother, whom we love, is sitting right here in this chair together with us."

LEARN FROM YOUR CRITICS

The book of James talks about those who carry leadership being called to a higher standard. This is especially true in the area of communication. A leader's words of correction can penetrate much more deeply, sometimes resulting in wounding. Likewise, their words of praise can do much to encourage people toward their best.

One thing is for sure: if you carry some sort of leadership role, people are never going to agree with everything you do. God has been speaking to me about how to graciously receive other people's "input" or "correction," because I can be too quick to react. If somebody gets their gun out and starts shooting me down, "You…you… you!" I can be very quick to pull my gun out and shoot back, "Well, but you…you…you!" Proverbs 19:11 says, *"A man's discretion makes him slow to anger, and it is his glory to overlook transgression"* (NASB).

In the early days on the UofN campus in Kona, I provided leadership over the operational areas. One day, a woman came to me and said, "I have seven things to talk to you about; five of them are negative and two of them are positive." She then proceeded to unload all seven of them, like a double-barreled shotgun. When she finished, I couldn't find the two positive things.

Prior to walking into that meeting, I had asked the Lord to help me, because I knew this woman was disgruntled. This is what He impressed upon me: I didn't have to answer right away; I was to hear her, take a step back, and respond by saying, "Thank you for caring enough about me to bring this to my attention. I know I have a great deal to learn. I will take these points to the Lord and ask Him to show me my heart."

As soon as the woman left, I quickly ran to God and cried, "Did you hear what that lady said about me? Is that true?" He gently replied, "Mm-hmm. A little bit." But God's conviction was so much easier to receive than her accusation.

TEETH MARKS ON MY TONGUE

It has been my meditation on Scriptures about communication that has put a conviction within me to seek to develop self-control.

When confronted with a frustrating situation, there is a quick grid of Scriptures that I think through. If I am aggravated with you over something and I know that I need to talk to you, I will seldom do it immediately, lest I fall prey to the emotion of the moment. *"Set a guard over my mouth, O Lord; keep watch over the door of my lips"* (Psalm 141:3 NIV).

It is so important from God's perspective that my words bring grace to you, not condemnation. If I ponder my response before the Lord, rather than just reacting in my flesh, God will give wisdom. *"Do not let any unwholesome talk come out of your mouths, but only what is helpful for building others up according to their needs, that it may benefit those who listen"* (Ephesians 4:29 NIV).

It is not that we are "vanilla" people or don't have an opinion about things—it's just that He has a standard for the way we communicate that is higher and will result in greater fruitfulness.

I sometimes have teeth marks on my tongue from choosing to have the self-control *not* to speak! Proverbs 10:19 says, *"When there are many words transgression is unavoidable, but he who restrains his lips is wise"* (NASB). I want to develop a higher standard, where the meditation of my heart and mind is the filter, not my teeth!

EXPRESSING GRATEFULNESS

Being full of integrity in communication also affects our expression of gratefulness to others. When I get praised for a job well done, true integrity motivates me to make sure everyone knows that I didn't do that job by myself. It's important for everyone who has contributed to the success of a project to be acknowledged and thanked.

In 2010, YWAM celebrated its fiftieth anniversary. As a part of that celebration, Loren and I traveled to forty-four locations in thirty-five different countries to meet together with approximately thirty thousand YWAMers, YWAM alumni, and YWAM friends to remember God's faithfulness in the past, celebrate His goodness in the present, and commit to "take the flame forward" into the future. The two of us received a tremendous amount of honor during that year-long anniversary, but the truth is, the only reason we looked good is because of all our wonderful YWAMers around the world who were doing such a great job of fulfilling our call: "To Know God and to Make Him Known." The more we traveled, the more grateful we became. As a part of those celebrations, together with the YWAMers gathered at each location, we thanked God for every pastor, parent, family, and friend who has served, prayed, and given to the mission throughout the years.

SPEAK THE TRUTH ABOUT GOD

Lastly, I want to talk about upholding God's character through your communication. He is always good, just, kind, loving, faithful…do our words line up with His Word?

Grumbling and complaining lead to unbelief…and they lead others toward unbelief, as well. We tend to grumble and complain when we look at isolated, difficult situations without seeing them in the light of who God is, as if everything were just left up to *my* understanding, *my* wisdom, *my* power. Yes, certainly we can tell God, "I'm disappointed; I'm hurt; I didn't think it would be like this." But what matters in the midst of difficult circumstances is who *God* is. Despite our own disappointment or hurt, we can know that God is trustworthy. And it's only as we look to Him that He can deliver us from the circumstances…or take us through them successfully.

In relationships, you can be a seed for unbelief through grumbling and complaining, or a seed for building faith by looking for God's faithfulness and identifying things to be grateful for.

Gratitude and faith go hand in hand. We see examples of this throughout God's Word. When we express gratefulness for who

God is and call to remembrance the great things He has done in the past, it gives us faith to believe Him for the present and the future. Just as the children of Israel stacked stones at the Jordan where God had proven His greatness (see Joshua 4:4–7), we need to stack stones of remembrance—stones of gratitude—in our lives and build them into our conversations, so that when others ask us, "What do these stones mean?" we can communicate the goodness and faithfulness of God.

FIVE

DICK EASTMAN

Going the Distance with Integrity

Dr. Dick Eastman is international president of Every Home for Christ (EHC), a 65-year-old ministry that has planted over three billion gospel messages home to home in 215 nations resulting in over 150 million follow-up decisions and responses. A staff of 8,000 supported workers and

45,000 monthly volunteers carry out the work of reaching an estimated 250,000 homes a day with the gospel. In his role with EHC, Dick has traveled around the world more than 100 times to every continent. He also serves as president of America's National Prayer Committee and is the author of numerous best-selling books on prayer and evangelism with more than three million copies in print. Dick's vision for greater cooperation in Christ's body for unified evangelism strategies across the globe has birthed The Jericho Center for Global Evangelism in Colorado Springs, Colorado, where 24/7 worship and intercession is also currently being developed.

It was late October and I was speaking at a conference involving several thousand young people. The nature of the conference was for the younger generation to hear from several spiritual fathers who were asked to speak into their generation, offering insights to help them "go the distance" in their walk with Jesus.

I must confess that I feel a bit uncomfortable being introduced so reverently as a spiritual father, other than the fact I recognize God has blessed my wife and me with a joyful ministry stretching over five decades. But if that means there might be something of encouragement from our journey that we could pass on to a younger generation, we are happy to share it.

Early in my message that evening, I referenced the life of the prophet Samuel, highlighting a phrase that particularly stood out to me about Samuel's life: *"Everyone in Israel, from Dan in the north to Beersheba in the south, recognized that Samuel was the real thing—a true prophet of God"* (1 Samuel 3:20 MSG).

I was challenging the many hundreds of young people present that night to be the "real deal" for Jesus in their walk with Him. Being the real deal was key, as I suggested, to going the distance for Christ in our lives and ministries. How easy it is to mask our deficiencies, often hidden from everyone but ourselves and God! Years ago I read that Francis of Assisi, when visiting groups of his spiritual brothers in the early 1200s (those who eventually would be labeled Franciscans), would end his visits with the same verbal good-bye: "My brothers, remember as I bid you farewell—what a man is before God, that he is, and no more!"

WORMY FRUIT

When we begin our journey for Jesus—and this is especially true for those who feel called to ministry leadership in some capacity—two things often flood our thinking. For one, we want somehow to be useful to the Lord in whatever way He chooses that might bring Him glory. Said simply, we want to be successful for Jesus. Second, we want to finish what we start and do so honorably. In other words, we want to "go the distance" and "finish well"!

Those are certainly worthy goals in and of themselves. But there can be a danger in this process, especially at the beginning, depending on our view of "success." Jack Hayford reminds us, "Success is not always an indication of significance." Mother Teresa adds, "God didn't call me to be successful. He called me to be faithful."

A. W. Tozer concludes, "God may allow His servant to succeed when He has disciplined him to a point where he does not need to succeed to be happy. The man who is elated by success and is cast down by failure is still a carnal man. At best his fruit will have a worm in it."[9]

None of us wants to finish life's journey with wormy fruit. And that's why I'm encouraged by the overall theme of this book. We want to be the *real deal*, full of integrity and truth, to go the distance for our wonderful Lord and, in the end, finish well.

---

9. A. W. Tozer, *Born After Midnight*, (Chicago, IL: Moody Publishers, reprinted 2015, originally published by Christian Publications, 1959). https://books.google.com/book s?id=koSICgAAQBAJ&pg=PT2&lpg=PT2&dq=#v=onepage&q&f=false

TRUTH BE TOLD

In a court of law, witnesses are placed under oath and admonished to declare they will tell "the whole truth and nothing but the truth, so help me God." Most also are familiar with the idiom "truth be told." It's an expression used when admitting something one might otherwise be dishonest about (what we sometimes refer to as "white lies") in order to keep up appearances or just to be polite. For example, one might say, "Actually, truth be told, I just don't like our worship leader's style of music."

Truth, by definition, is conformity to fact or actuality. It is also defined as a "comprehensive statement that in all of its nuances implies accuracy and honesty."[10] Herman Bavinck explains, "When we ascribe metaphysical 'truth' to an object or a person, we mean that that object or person is all that it is supposed to be. In that sense, gold which is gold not only in appearance but in reality, is real, pure, 'true' gold."[11] It is, quite simply, the real deal.

The author of Proverbs penned: *"Buy the truth, and sell it not"* (Proverbs 23:23 KJV). Jesus said, *"And you shall know the truth, and the truth shall make you free"* (John 8:32). Christ even described Himself as *"the way, the truth, and the life"* (John 14:6). These verses are all familiar to most Christ-followers. Truth is important.

During the weeks and months after sharing with the youth at that conference about being the "real deal," I couldn't shake the feeling that our ministry, Every Home for Christ (EHA), needed to discuss this topic of truthfulness and integrity with our many leaders throughout the world. As EHA's sixty-fifth anniversary approached, I meditated on it in further depth and put together three primary goals followed by what I refer to as an acronym of accountability.

---

10. "Truth," *American Heritage 5th Edition Dictionary*, https://www.ahdictionary.com/word/search.html?q=truth&submit.x=60&submit.y=22.

11. Herman Bavinck, *The Doctrine of God* (Grand Rapids, MI: Baker, 1977), 201.

GOAL #1: WALK THE WALK

It is deeply disheartening when we discover that leaders we have highly esteemed and admired have, in actuality, been living a double standard. Sadly, their behavior, when it becomes public, often erases years of sometimes amazingly fruitful ministry. I recall speaking at a well-known megachurch years ago and seeing an elaborate bookstore filled with stack after stack of books written by their popular pastor, along with sets of CDs and DVDs of his sermons. Later I visited that same church soon after this pastor had resigned his position due to an immorality that had been going on for several years. Every book, CD, and DVD by that once-popular pastor was gone. It was a ghost bookstore. Books and CDs of other authors and Christian musicians that had been on the shelves previously were now conspicuously spread out to fill all the empty display spaces. It was sad. For all practical purposes, it appeared as if that pastor had never been there at all.

On another occasion, a young pastor told me of a trip he had taken to a filming session of a popular televangelist. This fledgling pastor had a college friend who was working on the production staff of this televangelist's widely viewed weekly television program and had invited the pastor to sit quietly in the shadows to view the production of a month's worth of the evangelist's TV shows. This pastor considered this privilege to be in special honor of his young, emerging ministry, but the famous TV evangelist in reality had no idea the young pastor was sitting out of view.

During the filming of the first program, the evangelist ended by making a stirring emotional appeal for funds, stating that his ministry needed more than a million dollars in the coming thirty days, or he would have to cancel contracts with numerous stations due to lack of funds. Then, during a brief break of some ten or fifteen minutes the evangelist changed his wardrobe in preparation for filming the second program. At the end of that taping the evangelist shared the need once again, but added: "Last week I shared that we needed one million dollars in the next thirty days or we would have to go off the air in many markets, and I want to thank those of you who responded. Praise God, you have responded generously by sending almost $200,000, so we're on our way to a miracle. But I need many more of you to give if we are to see a total victory by the end of the month."

The young pastor saw this same dishonest approach used for the conclusions of the additional tapings; each time, the evangelist ended with a new appeal that included an update of how much money had come in the mail that specific week. Finally, he watched the evangelist change his wardrobe a one last time to do the concluding taping for the month's broadcasts. As that taping ended, the evangelist ended the program by proclaiming, "Praise God! Your gifts this past month have given us a true miracle! With your generous support we have reached our goal of the million dollars needed this month." The evangelist added, "Please, please continue to stand with us for our needs during the coming weeks and months. We need you now more than ever!" My young pastor friend was devastated by the hypocrisy and quietly exited the studio.

He had watched one of the most revered leaders he had known demonstrate on recorded television the precise opposite of what it means to "walk the walk."

I would be remiss if failed to share a positive example of one who "walked the walk." One of the most inspirational motion pictures to ever come out of Hollywood was the Academy Award-winning movie *Chariots of Fire*, released in 1981. It was the story of the star Scottish athlete, twenty-two-year-old Eric Liddell, whose athletic skills earned him the nickname "The Flying Scotsman."

The son of Scottish missionaries serving with the London Missionary Society in eastern China, Liddell was actually born in China in 1902. He, along with his brother Robert, was enrolled in Eltham College, Mottingham, a boarding school for missionary children in south London, when only six years old. As he grew, Liddell became an outstanding athlete; by the time he went to the university, he was a star rugby player and an excellent sprinter and long-distance runner.

In 1923, Liddell won the AAA British Championships' 100-yard dash in 9.7 seconds, setting a British record that stood for twenty-three years. It made Liddell the odds-on favorite to win the gold medal in the 1924 Paris Olympic Games in the 100-meter race. But Liddell refused to run. The match was set for a Sunday, and Eric Liddell decline to participate in sports activities on the Sabbath. He went to church instead. (In a subsequent 400-meter race, however, not on a Sunday, Liddell did win a gold medal.)

Such conduct was an integral part of Eric Liddell's fierce commitment to "walk the walk" in accordance with his biblical convictions. Indeed, while studying at Eltham College years earlier, Liddell's headmaster described Eric as being "entirely without vanity." True to his convictions that his real calling was to be a missionary, Eric Liddell returned to China in 1925, where he served as a missionary until his death in a Japanese internment camp in 1945. Eric Liddell truly embodied a "walk the walk" lifestyle.

Paul told believers at Galatia, *"But I say, walk by the Spirit, and you will not carry out the desire of the flesh"* (Galatians 5:16 NASB). John added: *"He who says he abides in [Christ] ought himself also to walk just as He walked"* (1 John 2:6). A life of integrity, indeed, is to walk the walk!

GOAL #2: RUN THE RACE

Scripture likewise pictures our journey in life as a race to be run, focusing on finishing well and winning. The apostle Paul admonished believers at Corinth:

Don't you realize that in a race everyone runs, but only one person gets the prize? So run to win! All athletes are disciplined

*in their training. They do it to win a prize that will fade away,
but we do it for an eternal prize. So I run with purpose in
every step. I am not just shadowboxing. I discipline my body
like an athlete, training it to do what it should. Otherwise, I
fear that after preaching to others I myself might be disquali-
fied.*   (1 Corinthians 9:24–27 NLT)

Recently while speaking to a gathering of our ministry leadership from across the Pacific Islands, I quoted powerful timeless
statements from the likes of past giants of the faith such as Dwight
L. Moody, Dr. A. T. Pierson, E. M. Bounds, and R. A. Torrey. Let
me tell you a bit about these men.

Dwight L. Moody, whom I have a special respect for, was
the Billy Graham of his generation and impacted millions with
his anointed messages. Those messages continue speaking today,
in print, impacting multitudes more. I had the joy of attending
the Bible college Moody founded, the Moody Bible Institute in
Chicago.

R. A. Torrey, a close friend of Moody, was a remarkable
evangelist in his own right and one of the founding leaders of the
Bible Institute of Los Angeles in the early 1900s, which continues
today as Biola University in California, one of the greatest evangelical Christian institutions of our day. Torrey had entered Yale
University at the young age of fifteen and ultimately graduated
with two degrees. But most importantly, in his third year at Yale,
this brilliant young man received Christ as Savior. EHA has dis-
tributed thousands of Torrey's books overseas to follow-up with
new believers, especially his classic, and very helpful, book on the
Holy Spirit.

Dr. A. T. Pierson, a Presbyterian pastor and Bible teacher, was
used by God to impact thousands of young people to go to the mission fields in the late 1800s and early 1900s. Pierson preached over
13,000 sermons and authored more than fifty books. Although
Pierson was American, he is perhaps best known for being the

successor to Charles H. Spurgeon's pulpit when Spurgeon retired from the Metropolitan Tabernacle of London in 1891.

E. M. Bounds, a Missouri-born attorney during America's Civil War, went on to write some of the most remarkable books ever written on the need for, and power of, fervent prayer. Amazingly only two of Bounds' eleven books were published before he died. His books *Power Through Prayer* and *Purpose in Prayer* are true classics. Bounds died in 1913 but his legacy of praying with power lives on.

As I quoted from each of these remarkable leaders to a young generation of our Pacific leadership team, I couldn't help but pause to highlight the fact that I was quoting from men who, although dead and gone for at least a century, were still affecting lives. Their words lived on. What was their secret? They all had one quality in common: they ran life's race faithfully and finished well. True, they had their critics and they had their faults. But because of how they lived and how they finished, they continue to preach and teach with undiminished impact. I wonder sometimes if past leaders in that heavenly sphere can look down upon those of us still in the race, urging us on. Perhaps this is what the author of Hebrews was thinking of this when he wrote:

> *Therefore, since we are surrounded by such a huge crowd of witnesses to the life of faith, let us strip off every weight that slows us down, especially the sin that so easily trips us up. And let us run with endurance the race God has set before us. We do this by keeping our eyes on Jesus, the champion who initiates and perfects our faith. Because of the joy awaiting him, he endured the cross, disregarding its shame. Now he is seated in the place of honor beside God's throne.*
>
> (Hebrews 12:1–2 NLT)

All of this continues to relate to our being the real deal and finishing well. Paul, in his writings to Roman believers, highlighted these worthy goals while also challenging them to avoid burnout:

Love from the center of who you are; don't fake it. Run for
dear life from evil; hold on for dear life to good. Be good
friends who love deeply; practice playing second fiddle. Don't
burn out; keep yourselves fueled and aflame. Be alert servants
of the Master, cheerfully expectant. Don't quit in hard times;
pray all the harder....   (Romans 12:9–13 MSG)

To all those who may have stumbled in their walk—don't give
up! As Paul said, *"Don't quit in hard times"* but rather *"pray all the*
harder." A mark of integrity is to keep running, true to your original intention, without succumbing to burnout.

GOAL #3: FIGHT THE FIGHT

I first met Reggie White, NFL Hall of Fame defensive end,
at a meeting of a handful of leaders who had gathered in the foot-
hills of North Carolina to pray together and share together about
our nation's future. We wanted to hear prophetically what the
Lord might be saying regarding trends in our declining American
culture.

Standing alone in the entry to the lodge prior to the start
of the retreat, I was suddenly startled by a towering man standing directly behind me. I turned to hear him say, "Hi, I'm Reggie
White; you wouldn't happen to have six Advil on you, would you?"
It was a strange introduction, but I quickly learned he had come
from a Carolina Panthers' game just two days earlier. Reggie spent
his final year playing for the Panthers, after spending his early
years with the Philadelphia Eagles and later his most successful
days as a Green Bay Packer, which, as Wisconsin-born, I claim as
my team. (And no, I didn't happen to be carrying six Advil on me
that day.)

During our times of sharing as a group for the next several
days, various leaders related something of their individual stories.
Reggie White, a twelve-time All-Pro and thirteen-time All-Pro

selection to the Pro Bowl, particularly shared about what it takes to be a champion, fighting through whatever pain happens to be necessary in order to win. Nicknamed "the Minister of Defense," Reggie's football expertise as an NFL defensive end, coupled with his strong Christian faith demonstrated in everyday life, resulted in a continuous fight both on the field and off. He was, for example, denied a very lucrative television contract after he retired from the NFL simply because of his outspoken stance on the definition of marriage as being between a man and a woman. He simply wouldn't compromise his convictions.

There's little doubt Reggie White would have made one of the great football commentators of our century. Sadly, he passed away at the young age of forty-three in December 2004. One statement of his has always stuck with me, considering his incredible character: "God places the heaviest burden on those who can carry its weight." An unknown sage adds, "Don't pray for lighter burdens, but for stronger backs." Corrie ten Boom, who risked her life during World War II hiding Jews from the Nazis (as memorialized in her book and subsequent movie *The Hiding Place*), suggests, "If God sends us on strong paths, we are provided strong shoes."

Indeed, those who surrender their lives as Christ-followers soon learn they are engaged in ongoing spiritual warfare. Paul admonished Timothy, *"Fight the good fight of faith, lay hold on eternal life, to which you were also called and have confessed the good confession in the presence of many witnesses"* (1 Timothy 6:12). As his life neared its earthly end, Paul would pen one of his most memorable reflections:

> *I have fought the good fight, I have finished the race, I have kept the faith. Finally, there is laid up for me the crown of righteousness, which the Lord, the righteous Judge, will give to me on that Day, and not to me only but also to all who have loved His appearing.* (2 Timothy 4:7–8)

Of course, our fight is never a struggle absent of personal suffering and often requires a healthy measure of spiritual endurance. The apostle Peter advised:

> *Beloved, do not think it strange concerning the fiery trial which is to try you, as though some strange thing happened to you; but rejoice to the extent that you partake of Christ's sufferings, that when His glory is revealed, you may also be glad with exceeding joy.... Yet if anyone suffers as a Christian, let him not be ashamed, but let him glorify God in this matter.... Therefore let those who suffer according to the will of God commit their souls to Him in doing good, as to a faithful Creator.*
>
> (1 Peter 4:12–13, 16, 19)

Maltbie Davenport Babcock offers this wise conclusion to our "fight the fight" goal:

> "Blessed is the man that endureth temptation, for when he is tried he shall receive the crown of life, which the Lord hath promised to them that love him.' It is a verse of climbing power. It begins with man, it ends with God. It begins with earth, it ends with heaven. It begins with struggle, it ends with a crown.... Blessed is the man that endureth, stands up under it, resists, conquers. "Blessed," for it means new wisdom, new strength, new joy, and "the crown of life."[12]

Fighting, not just enduring, has been a mark of integrity in faith leaders through the centuries.

AN ACRONYM OF ACCOUNTABILITY

In addressing Corinthian believers on a key qualification for spiritual leadership, Paul wrote: *"Moreover it is required in stewards*

---

12. Maltbie Davenport Babcock, quoted in *Thoughts for Every-Day Living from the Spoken and Written Words of Maltbie Davenport Babcock* (New York: C. Scribner's, 1901), 92–93.

that one be found faithful" (1 Corinthians 4:2). The NIV translates this, "*Now it is required that those who have been given a trust must prove faithful.*" The NLT suggests, "*Now, a person who is put in charge as a manager must be faithful.*" I especially like the rendering of the *Amplified* version: "*Moreover, it is [essentially] required of stewards that a man should be found faithful [proving himself worthy of trust].*"

Reflecting on all that accountability involves, and our continuing fight to maintain a godly, faithful walk in Christ, the Lord led me to Paul's great chapter on spiritual warfare, Ephesians 6. I was especially stirred as I read the rendering in *The Message*, verse 12: "*This is no afternoon athletic contest that we'll walk away from and forget about in a couple of hours. This is for keeps, a life-or-death fight to the finish against the Devil and all his angels*" (Ephesians 6:12). Meditating long and hard on all aspects of the armor, Paul admonishes us to put on for the battles that lay ahead, I was particularly drawn to Paul's words of verse 13:

> *Be prepared. You're up against far more than you can handle on your own. Take all the help you can get, every weapon God has issued, so that when it's all over but the shouting you'll still be on your feet.* (Ephesians 6:13 MSG)

A particularly significant part of this passage stood out to me that I felt was a special caution to those in spiritual leadership. It included Paul's words in verse fourteen: "*Stand therefore, having your loins girt about with truth*" (KJV). The *Amplified* version's translation of this admonition reads: "*Stand therefore [hold your ground], having tightened the belt of truth around your loins and having put on the breastplate of integrity and of moral rectitude and right standing with God.…*"

It was the word "*loins*" that captured my attention in this passage. Paul admonished us to "tighten the belt of truth" around our "loins." The word "*loins*" is defined as "the region of the hips, groin, and lower abdomen including the reproductive organs." As I reflected on the fact that the area of the hips represents the area of our capacity to reproduce, and the area of many of our most vital organs as well as a source for temptation, an interesting symbolism occurred to me. Four qualities of leadership emerged creating the acronym HIPS. The more I considered these four qualities, the more I realized they are clearly foundational to the character of a truly godly leader (or any believer, for that matter) who aspires to be full of integrity.

Humility

Pride, without a doubt, is the primary enemy of effective, godly leadership. The familiar words of Proverbs 16:18 ring true: *"Pride goes before destruction, and haughtiness before a fall"* (NLT). *The Message's* paraphrase of Proverbs 16:8 is more blunt: *"First pride, then the crash—the bigger the ego, the harder the fall."*

Humility, of course, is pride's antonym (its opposite). Paul spoke of this quality called humility as he cautioned (even begged) Christians at Ephesus to walk worthy of the calling God had given each of them:

> *I therefore, the prisoner for the Lord, appeal to and beg you to walk (lead a life) worthy of the [divine] calling to which you have been called [with behavior that is a credit to the summons to God's service, living as becomes you] with complete lowliness of mind (humility) and meekness (unselfishness, gentleness, mildness), with patience, bearing with one another and making allowances because you love one another.*
>
> (Ephesians 4:1–2 AMP)

Indeed, Paul didn't just speak of an ordinary humility (if there is such a thing) but of *"complete lowliness of mind (humility)."* Note the word *"complete."* Augustine wrote: "Humility is the foundation of all the other virtues, hence, in the soul in which this virtue does not exist there cannot be any other virtue except in mere appearance."[13] I like Rick Warren's insight on humility: "This is

---

13. See http://www.egs.edu/library/augustine-of-hippo/quotes/.

true humility: not thinking less of ourselves, but thinking of ourselves less."[14]

Andrew Murray wrote:

Humility, the place of entire dependence on God, is, from the very nature of things, the first duty and the highest virtue of man. It is the root of every virtue.... Humility is the only soil in which the graces take root; the lack of humility is the sufficient explanation of every defect and failure. Humility is not so much a grace or virtue along with others; it is the root of all, because it alone assumes the right attitude before God and allows Him as God to do all.[15]

In Proverbs we read: *"Fear-of-God is a school in skilled living— first you learn humility then you experience glory"* (Proverbs 15:33 MSG). Later in Proverbs we read: *"Pride lands you flat on your face; humility prepares you for honors"* (Proverbs 29:23 MSG). I especially like the paraphrase of James 1:21 in *The Message*: *"In simple humility, let our gardener, God, landscape you with the Word, making a salvation-garden of your life."*

May those who are called to Christian leadership seek in every way a spirit of humility, while remembering the words of an unknown prophetic voice: "Humility can be sought but never celebrated."

Integrity

I laughed with all the others in the auditorium after the guest speaker told a stirring story, possibly with a bit of exaggeration, and then jokingly added: "I've never told a story that God couldn't do!" That is certainly true, but oh, that God would caution us in

14. Rick Warren, *The Purpose-Driven Life* (Grand Rapids, MI: Zondervan, 2002), "Day 19."
15. Andrew Murray, *Humility* (New Kensington, PA: Whitaker House, 1982), 16–17.

how we recount His blessings. Do we exaggerate the details here and there, just to enhance the story?

Again, the author of Proverbs has a word of caution to say about this: *"A good and honest life is a blessed memorial"* (Proverbs 10:7 MSG) and *"The integrity of the honest keeps them on track"* (Proverbs 11:3 MSG). Still later in Proverbs we read: *"An honest life shows respect for God"* (Proverbs 14:2 MSG). Luke would much later record these words of Jesus: *"If you're honest in small things, you'll be honest in big things…"* (Luke 16:10 MSG).

Integrity, indeed, is an essential ingredient to godly character and effective leadership. Joy Dawson, long associated as a key voice in the early days of the impactful Youth With A Mission (YWAM) movement, often cautioned, "Exaggeration is nothing but a flowery lie." The popular Yiddish Proverb adds: "A half-truth is a whole lie." Oh, for a movement of single-minded integrity!

Integrity is defined as "steadfast adherence to a strict moral or ethical code" and "the state or condition of being whole or undivided; completeness."[16] The word "steadfast" particularly stands out in this definition. Beloved reader, cultivate the courage to defend what is right and confront what is wrong. Seek to live an integrity-saturated life. I so admired the steadfastness of the David Green family of Oklahoma City, Oklahoma, owners of Hobby Lobby, during their stand against providing employees contraceptives that are known to potentially cause abortion. Their case went all the way to the US Supreme Court and was ultimately decided in favor of the Green family in late June 2014. Some believe it was one of the most significant religious liberty cases in the history of America's highest court. The Greens literally wrestled with closing down their billion dollar company rather than bowing to government requirements that they felt to be contrary to God's Word. The required fines, if they had lost their case, could well have totaled more than $365 million a year (at least a million dollars or

---

16. "Integrity," http://www.thefreedictionary.com/integrity (accessed July 14, 2015).

more daily). It would have been an amount clearly unsustainable for their corporation. But, praise God, they were victorious! What a rich legacy the Greens have left for other marketplace leaders and believers who likewise hold deep-rooted biblical convictions.

Purity

"*Blessed are the pure in heart: for they shall see God*" (Matthew 5:8 KJV). *The Message* offers this paraphrase for the same verse: "*You're blessed when you get your inside world—your mind and heart—put right. Then you can see God in the outside world.*" Purity is putting right your inside world—a natural result of a life of integrity that destroys disparity in holiness between the "inside world" and the "outside world."

The apostle Paul addressed this subject of purity in our thoughts and actions in his second letter to Corinthian believers. He wrote: "*Because we have these promises, dear friends, let us cleanse ourselves from everything that can defile our body or spirit. And let us work toward complete holiness because we fear God*" (2 Corinthians 7:1 NLT). *The Message* paraphrases this passage, saying, "*With promises like this to pull us on, dear friends, let's make a clean break with everything that defiles or distracts us, both within and without.*" The interesting thought in this passage is that we (the believer) are the ones who need to cleanse our hearts. Note the phrase "*let us cleanse ourselves.*" Years ago, in teaching youth of our need to cultivate purity in our lives, I referred to this passage as God's "Broom Principle." I suggested that God is our great Forgiver (He will forgive all our sins), but He also hands us a spiritual broom (of sorts). He does the forgiving, but we must do the sweeping.

Paul is clearly speaking here of living a life of purity before our Lord. Describing such purity, Rachel Hamilton suggests:

Purity is not a set of boundaries and rules that one must follow, not a legalistic word that binds us up, making us afraid to venture into the impure world. No, purity is falling so in love with Christ that we want our lives to mirror His. Purity should bloom from obedience to Christ, wanting to make Him proud. There is freedom in purity; for when we seek His heart, it is there that His guidance and wisdom are found.[17]

When writing my first book on prayer, *No Easy Road*, and describing what I felt holiness embodied as it related to a life of prayer, I suggested that holiness is not an ever-continuing compilation of a list of dos and don'ts, but rather it is the experience of the believer falling so in love with Jesus that no list is ever needed.

In the murky climate of today's declining moral culture there is little doubt that God is calling His people, and particularly leaders of His people, to a new life of moral and ethical purity. And from that purity, may God lead us to a new simplicity.

Simplicity

"One of the purest souls ever to live on this fallen planet," wrote A. W. Tozer, "was Nicholas Herman...known as Brother Lawrence." Tozer goes on to explain,

> He wrote very little, but what he wrote has seemed to several generations of Christians to be so rare and so beautiful as to deserve a place near the top among the world's great books of devotion.... The writings of Brother Lawrence are the ultimate in simplicity...ideas woven like costly threads to make a pattern of beauty.[18]

There is something powerful about living a life of simplicity as a follower of Christ. Brother Lawrence lived that life of "ultimate simplicity." How do we pursue such a life? John wrote, "*Love not*

---

17. Rachel Hamilton, *Hidden Struggles: Purity, God, Guys & Love* (Bloomington, IN: Westbow Press, 2013).
18. A. W. Tozer, *The Price of Neglect and Other Essays* (Camp Hill, PA: Wingspread Publishers, 1991, e-book).

the world, neither the things that are in the world" (1 John 2:15 KJV). One legendary story about John Wesley goes like this: Once when Wesley was preaching a sermon on the world, someone shouted from the crowd, "Wesley, what do you mean by 'the world?'" Wesley supposedly replied: "Anything that cools my affection for Jesus is the world!" An absence of *things* is clearly the first step to creating an atmosphere of simplicity. Beloved reader, cultivate a *thing-less* life.

Simplicity, in a sense, is something of a first cousin to humility, bringing my acronym full-circle. The humblest are often the simplest and the simplest the humblest. Note the instructions Jesus gave His disciples when He commissioned them to take His good news to the lost:

> *Jesus called the Twelve to him, and sent them out in pairs. He gave them authority and power to deal with the evil opposition. He sent them off with these instructions: "Don't think you need a lot of extra equipment for this. You are the equipment. No special appeals for funds. Keep it simple."... Then they were on the road. They preached with joyful urgency that life can be radically different.*   (Mark 6:7–9, 12 MSG)

Having just enough is to have enough.

Paul's ministry carried on Jesus' instruction to the twelve and embodied simplicity. He said of his calling:

> *You'll remember, friends, that when I first came to you to let you in on God's master stroke, I didn't try to impress you with polished speeches and the latest philosophy. I deliberately kept it plain and simple: first Jesus and who he is; then Jesus and what he did—Jesus crucified.*   (1 Corinthians 2:2 MSG)

Cultivate *simplicity* (quite simply!) by rejecting complexity. It's as *simple* as that (pun intended)! Oh, for the grace to recognize complexity! A wise mentor told me early in my ministry, "God's plans are almost always simple and inexpensive. So, if things get complicated and expensive, it may be good to rethink your strategy."

Humility, integrity, purity, simplicity: pursue all four of these worthy qualities with a righteous jealousy. And in your pursuit, walk the walk, run the race, and fight the fight. God wants you to finish well—and to win. He likewise wants you to finish faithfully and fruitfully. And I believe I can promise you with an absolute certainty that in the end, God will always be answering. I imagine He is even speaking to you just now!

SIX

STACEY CAMPBELL

The Lost Heart of Integrity in Marriage

S*tacey Campbell is a prophetic voice to this generation and has a passion to teach believers to know how to hear the voice of God through proper teaching and strong values. She is the founder and facilitator of the Canadian Prophetic Council and serves as an honorary member of the Apostolic Council* *of Prophetic Elders, presided over by Dr. Peter Wagner and Cindy Jacobs. Stacey is on the apostolic team of Harvest International Ministries (HIM) under Ché Ahn. Stacey and her husband Wesley are founders of New Life Church in Kelowna, British Columbia, and a mercy organization for children at risk called Be a Hero. As conference speakers, both Stacey and Wesley have ministered in over sixty nations, laboring to see revival and social justice transform the world. Their personal experience as missionaries, church planters, and pastors gives their teaching a depth and authority that can only come from personal experience. The Campbells have five grown children and live in Kelowna, British Columbia, Canada.*

I recently returned home from a national prayer meeting in the nation of Brazil. Leaders from across the nation met to seek the face of God—to get His perspective on the growing crisis in their country. The Spirit of God moved on us very deeply as God filled us with His sorrow about the corruption in the land. The nation was about to explode because of the disparity corruption had caused between the rich and the poor. In the streets, people were boiling with anger, threatening to override law and order. At the root of this national angst was a systemic loss of integrity. It seems that only revival—or revolution—will shift it.

Sadly, Brazil is not the only nation with an almost wholesale loss of integrity. The sexual revolution of the sixties has produced a harvest of divorce, abortion, homosexuality, and collapse of the family unit in North America as well. Commitment has given way to convenience and expediency. The church has largely failed to stem the demise of morality because we have tended to become critics of the sin, rather than coaches on how to overcome it. We have many teachers, but not many fathers. (See 1 Corinthians 4:15.) The restoration of financial and sexual integrity demands much more than lectures. Our culture's current depravity can only be changed by living epistles, by spiritual mothers and fathers modeling healthy marriages as well as speaking into and giving our lives to a generation inundated with bad examples.

The good news is that it is possible to live a life of integrity even in the worst possible conditions. Daniel showed us that. (See Daniel 1:8.) Joseph modeled it. (See Genesis 39:7–15.) John the Baptist preached it from the desert where he exhorted people to repent and flee the corruption of the day. (See Matthew 3.) These patriarchs showed us that, since integrity starts in the heart, it is possible to maintain integrity no matter what the outward conditions are. Jesus confirmed that the issue is not what is happening in the society around us, but rather what is happening in the heart. We are to guard our hearts with all diligence because sin is conceived from within. (See Matthew 23:25–28; Luke 21:34–36; James 1:13–15.)

INTEGRITY IS A CHOICE

Integrity is both lost and gained choice by choice. Little by little, our small decisions either draw us further and further away from holiness or closer and closer to righteousness. It is not by one great feat that integrity is attained. It is a thousand little, seemingly insignificant, steps that add up to a life of integrity. The principle spills over into every area and every attitude. A lifestyle of a long obedience in the same direction produces a heart that is faithful.

Nowhere is integrity needed more today than in marriages. A generation ago, it was a difficult and arduous process to get a divorce. The ramifications, socially and financially, were extensive. Divorcees were a minority. But when Ronald Reagan passed the "no fault divorce" bill in 1969, the floodgates of divorce were opened.

In the decade and a half that followed, virtually every state in the Union followed California's lead and enacted a no-fault divorce law of its own. This legal transformation was only one of the more visible signs of the divorce revolution then sweeping the United States: From 1960 to 1980, the divorce rate more than doubled — from 9.2 divorces per 1,000 married women to 22.6 divorces per 1,000 married women. This meant that while less than 20% of couples who married in 1950 ended up divorced, about 50% of couples who married in 1970 did. And approximately half of the children born to married parents in the 1970s saw their parents part, compared to only about 11% of those born in the 1950s.[19]

As we see from these statistics, somewhere between the bliss of romance and the wedding and the end-game of divorce, the institution of marriage has undergone a wholesale loss of integrity. The biblical injunction that *"marriage is to be held in honor among all, and the marriage bed is to be undefiled"* (Hebrews 13:4 NASB) no longer carries much weight. Something as trivial as "falling out of love" is seen as a viable cause for divorce. Many modern wedding vows now state that the participants pledge to be married "as long as our love shall last," instead of "till death do us part." When feelings override commitment, how can marital integrity be built?

I think there is a way to build integrity in marriage, and it is found in a shift of accent, in a commitment to the blessing of giving, in acknowledging the greatness of servanthood. Jesus taught us that *"it is more blessed to give than to receive"* (Acts 20:35 NASB) and that *"whoever wants to be first must take last place and be the servant of everyone else"* (Mark 9:35 NLT). When we practice giving and servanthood with those we are married to, we are really demonstrating kingdom marriage, the kind that Jesus demonstrates with His bride. Let's look at Ephesians 5 to understand how that works:

---

19. W. Bradford Wilcox, "The Evolution of Divorce," *National Affairs*, no. 1 (Fall 2009), http://www.nationalaffairs.com/publications/detail/the-evolution-of-divorce (accessed July 28, 2014).

Submit to one another out of reverence for Christ. For wives, this means submit to your husbands as to the Lord. For a husband is the head of his wife as Christ is the head of the church. He is the Savior of his body, the church. As the church submits to Christ, so you wives should submit to your husbands in everything. For husbands, this means love your wives, just as Christ loved the church. He gave up his life for her to make her holy and clean, washed by the cleansing of God's word. He did this to present her to himself as a glorious church without a spot or wrinkle or any other blemish. Instead, she will be holy and without fault. In the same way, husbands ought to love their wives as they love their own bodies. For a man who loves his wife actually shows love for himself. No one hates his own body but feeds and cares for it, just as Christ cares for the church.... This is a great mystery, but it is an illustration of the way Christ and the church are one. So again I say, each man must love his wife as he loves himself, and the wife must respect her husband.   (Ephesians 5:21–29, 32–33 NLT)

The desire for a good marriage increases when we contemplate what Christ intended marriage to be. These verses show us in a very practical way how we can maintain integrity in our primary covenantal relationship. The whole of Ephesians 5 is a love story. It marks the progression from being dearly loved children to living a life of love—the giving kind of love that Jesus demonstrated; a holy kind of love that pursues purity, even of speech. The standard for every believer seen in the beginning verses of Ephesians 5 becomes especially exemplified in marriage in the later verses of this same chapter. Nothing demonstrates the relationship that Christ has with His church like a Christian marriage.

In a Christian marriage, *the initiator of love is the husband*, who loves his wife and takes responsibility for bringing her blameless to the Lord, imitating the sacrificial love of Jesus. In response, the wife respects and submits to a husband who loves her that deeply.

It is a perfect model. The headship that the man has in marriage is lived out in sacrificial, Christ-like giving. Christ *gave* Himself. This is headship. This is the foundation of love, as modeled by Jesus. Headship looks like a sacrificial giving of yourself.

For the Christian husband who imitates Christ, *sacrifice will be central*. The husband leads by modeling sacrifice. The wife responds by respecting and honoring such an example of love. As these verses show, the Christian husband will empty himself to serve his wife. He will see her needs and anticipate what it will take to meet them. Like Christ, the husband's leadership has as its primary purpose to *"present her…without a spot or wrinkle or any other blemish"* (Ephesians 5:27 NLT). The husband is always asking, "What does it take to make my wife better?"

The Christian wife will return the sacrifice with respect and submission. This too is a central theological point: *"We love, because He first loved us"* (1 John 4:19 NASB). The bride responds to the love of the Bridegroom. Love in action begets love in response. To the Christian husband, I ask: "How are you leading in love?" Most often the leadership you give will determine the response you get. If you have a cranky wife, do you blame and withdraw? Or do you examine yourself and see if perhaps you have not served her needs well in this season of life? Are you expecting her to be the leader of love, and you the responder? This is not how headship works in marriage.

OUR STORY

Testing in relationships is normal and, like most couples, Wesley and I have been through some extremely hard seasons in our marriage. The pressures of ministry, family, and our own carnality take their toll. There was a time we invested all our money in a house that never got built, and lost every cent we had to our name. Another time, revival broke out, and it was the season to travel the world. We found ourselves traveling nonstop, moving every three days to a new ministry location...with five kids under the age of eight! Then there was the time we were fired, by our own friends, from our role as senior leaders of the church we planted. (I must note, however, that four years later the relationship was repaired, and we returned to the church.) If all that wasn't enough, in 2013 our son broke his neck and instantly became a quadriplegic. It was a long year to full recovery, yet now he is 100 percent healed.

These are the ups and downs of life. Added to these extraordinary events, we have faced the normal temptations of life. Though most of these trials were suddenly thrust upon us from without, each of them created abnormal stresses on our relationship with each other. It is easy to begin to blame the other person for the emotions that quickly rise when we are under pressure.

In fact, our first and biggest crisis of integrity happened only two months into our marriage. Wesley and I married very young. Wesley had been a missionary to Nigeria for an entire year while we were dating. He returned home when he was only twenty-one and, wanting to do the right thing, we married soon after, because we had already been going out for four years. When we married, I was two days shy of twenty and Wesley was a mere twenty-two.

Somehow, as the wedding day grew closer and closer, Wesley became cooler and cooler. He didn't really know how to process what he was feeling and what was going on inside. Later he understood that he was overwhelmed by the commitment. He was the first of all his friends to get married. The more nice things I did for him, the more he withdrew from me. Why? Because if he didn't feel like doing something nice back, he then felt obligated to do something that was not from his heart. It was a vicious spiral. After we married, I tried to do everything as lovingly as possible, as I thought a new wife should. But the more I did, the more Wesley went into a major funk. Then, on our two-month anniversary supper, Wesley spoke the words that crushed my spirit. He said, "I am sorry, Stacey—I am sorry for ruining your life. I think we have made a terrible mistake!"

I burst into tears. I was thinking, *This is what two months of marriage has brought us? My husband feeling like we made a terrible mistake in getting married?* We sat in silence for the next hour trying to eat our steak while tears ran down my cheeks. It didn't get any better for next few months. Wesley became even more distant. I felt even more hurt. Then, because we had planned it before we were married, we followed through with a second honeymoon to Southern California.

It was the days of Keith Green, of the Calvary Chapel revivals, and of the tail end of the Jesus Movement. We ended up in some sort of communal discipleship school and spent some days there. The spiritual atmosphere was thick and weighty. It was so much about God, about doing the right thing, about missions and evangelism. Being in that strong spiritual environment was good for both of us. One day when Wesley went to take a shower, God spoke to him. I will let Wesley relate his encounter to you in his own words:

> As I showered, the thought that I had made a terrible mistake kept going over and over in my mind. I said to myself, *I don't feel like I "love" Stacey. I just don't feel anything. What can I do?* I began to desperately pray, "God what should I do?"
>
> In an instant, and with unmistaken clarity, I heard the Scripture: "Husbands, love your wife as Christ loved the church." I knew I had heard from God. There was no getting around it. This was not about feelings or emotions. This was a categorical command from God Himself: "Wesley, you must love Stacey as Christ loved His own church." I knew I had to make decisions based on what I knew to be true, regardless of what my heart and flesh felt.

In fact, this was the same type of decision-making process I went through when I became a Christian.

So there, alone in the shower, with nothing but raw obedience as my motivation, I promised aloud to myself, "I will love my wife, Stacey, in the same way that Christ loved his church." It wasn't emotional. It wasn't based on anything that Stacey had done or had not done. It wasn't based on what I felt or did not feel. It was based on the Word of God—that called me as a husband to love my own wife. In the shower, before God, I said yes to Stacey that day.

I don't really know how it happened, but everything began to change after that. I prayed for emotions of love and I began to feel emotions of love again. I began to pray for Stacey and declare that she was the Proverbs 31 woman. Amazingly, soon after making the decision to love—to love like Christ loved the church—all my doubts and misgivings vanished. Within a very short time I felt happy to be married again. True love did come back. It was different than the early years when we were dating, but it was mature, beautiful love. I didn't feel any need to withhold and keep her at bay. I became happy to be married to Stacey.

Now thirty-five years later, I can't imagine our lives without each other. Sometimes I shudder to think what would have happened if I had listened to my feelings way back there in 1981 and not submitted myself to the will of God. Who knows where we would be right now. But as it is, we are happy. We have a great family of five children. We are rescuing hundreds and thousands of children at risk. And most of all—I really love Stacey!

AN OVERCOMING GENERATION

Christian leaders are to give themselves to the ministry of the Word and prayer. Compromise among Christian leaders often stems from the busyness of a successful ministry and the lack of a personal prayer life and study of the Word. (See Acts 6:4.) Usually it is not the pressures of adversity, but rather the pressures of success that cause most leaders to fall! This was true even in the life of David, a man who was diligently after God's own heart. (See Acts 13:22.) David got busy, then comfortable in his success, so that at a time when kings should have been going to war, he stayed home instead:

> *Then it happened in the spring,* **at the time when kings go out to** *battle, that Joab led out the army and ravaged the land of the sons of Ammon, and came and besieged Rabbah. But* **David stayed at Jerusalem....**   (1 Chronicles 20:1 NASB)

By not being where he should have been, with all his army fighting without him while he relaxed, David fell into adultery with Bathsheba. His guard was down. He had so much success. He had probably worn himself out with many battles, and they were on the upswing, so David stayed home. Neglecting his kingly duties, away from his men, he faced a new kind of battle—the battle of lust. That was a battle David lost. By not being in the right battle zone, he failed the moral test, and there were devastating consequences, even including the loss of his child. Similarly, when we lose the daily battle of giving ourselves to prayer and the ministry of the Word and stop disciplining ourselves to bring our own spiritual lives before God so we can lead by example from our own spirituality, we will probably lose the personal battles that will inevitably come before us.

Praying the Bible becomes a primary way to keep our ways pure.[20] (See Psalm 119:9.) The Bible washes our minds of the

---

20. For more information on how to pray the Bible, see *Praying the Bible: The Pathway to Spirituality* by Wesley & Stacey Campbell (Ventura, CA: Regal Publishing, 2002).

substandard morals of our cultures and raises us to lofty ideals and holy thoughts. Behavior comes out of belief. Fruit grows out of a root. When we are rooted and grounded in the knowledge of God, regularly setting our minds on things above, then our hearts are strengthened to respond rightly when the outward temptations of lust, anger, criticism, giving up—all that assails us.

I am personally deeply grieved at the lack of integrity in the marriages of Christian leaders. We regularly hear of pastors and wives who are unfaithful to each other—and no one even blinks. The pastors stay in the pulpits, bringing their new spouses into the ministry with them, sometimes within a matter of months. I want to say *sorry* to the younger generation: we have been poor models. But I call you to imitate those who imitate Christ! (See 1 Corinthians 11:1.) Find someone who is faithful, in word and in deed. For the sake of your own children, raise the standard of love in marriage once more.

For years, I have had revelation from the Lord that there will be an overcoming generation: a generation who will follow the Lord with their whole heart in spite of the evil around them. This generation will *"shine brightly like…the expanse of heaven, and…like stars forever and ever"* (Daniel 12:3 NASB). They will know their God and represent Him rightly. They will fix their eyes on Jesus and endure. (See Hebrews 12:2; 1 Peter 1:13–15.) Because they love Him, they will keep His commandments. (See John 14:15.) I believe that many from the next generation will make right what we have destroyed. So I look to the future with hope. Hope in a holy God who is able to keep us blameless (see Jude 1:24); hope in a generation that beholds Him longer and becomes more like Him (see 2 Corinthians 3:18); and, most of all, hope that this coming generation is the one that will seek His face and bring integrity back to the church (see Psalm 24:3–6).

SEVEN

CHÉ AHN

Financial Integrity

Ché Ahn and his wife, Sue, moved from the East Coast to Southern California in 1984 after receiving a dream of a revival outpouring in the greater Los Angeles area and eventually became the founding pastors of HRock Church in Pasadena, California. Ché is also the founder and president of Harvest International Ministry (HIM), a worldwide apostolic network of more than 25,000 churches in upwards *of sixty nations with the common vision to fulfill the Great Commandment and the Great Commission. He also serves as the international chancellor of Wagner Leadership Institute (WLI), an international network of apostolic training centers established to equip believers for kingdom ministry. With an MDiv and DMin from Fuller Theological Seminary, Ché has played a key role in many strategic outreaches on local, national, and international levels. He has written more than a dozen books and travels extensively throughout the world, bringing apostolic insight with an impartation of renewal, healing, and evangelism. Ché and Sue have four adult children and two amazing grandchildren.*

I once heard Billy Graham say the three greatest needs in the church are (1) integrity, (2) integrity, and (3) integrity. In many ways, that is a sad statement, but as a pastor for more than thirty-five years, I can say that is true—especially when it comes to financial integrity. Just look at recent issues of any Christian news magazine. *Christianity Today* recently published a story with a headline that leapt off the page and hit me in the gut: "Pastors Repay $1.2 Million in Diverted 9/11 Donations." The article explains how a pastoral couple of a major denomination embezzled $1.2 million donated for 9/11 and Hurricane Katrina victims and bought a brand-new BMW, a home in New Jersey, vacations to Florida, etc. The pastors got caught after an Associated Press investigation exposed the diverted funds, and their denomination forced them to repay that money. This story is a travesty to Christianity.

Jesus taught in Luke 16 that if you are faithful with money, God will give you true riches:

He who is faithful in a very little thing is faithful also in much; and he who is unrighteous in a very little thing is unrighteous also in much. Therefore if you have not been faithful in the use of unrighteous wealth, who will entrust the true riches to you? And if you have not been faithful in the use of that which is

another's, who will give you that which is your own? No ser-
vant can serve two masters; for either he will hate the one and
love the other, or else he will be devoted to one and despise the
other. You cannot serve God and wealth.

(Luke 16:10–13 NASB)

It's amazing how much the Bible says about money. Scripture contains more than 2,000 verses that have to do with money. Two thirds of Jesus' parables have to do with money. My mentor and spiritual father, Peter Wagner, has often said, "There are three things that have shaped our world. Number one is violence. Number two is knowledge. Number three is wealth, and the greatest is wealth." This is not a new Bible verse, but there is a great amount of truth to those words. Think about how wars and violence have shaped nations. Think about how knowledge and technology have changed our lives. But now think of how wealth impacts a nation. For example, just as I'm writing these words, 300 million Chinese are coming out of abject poverty and becoming middle-class citizens in China, and it's not because of a Christian organization or a UN program. It's because the economy is grow-ing so fast in China that hundreds of millions are being impacted by the growing wealth in their homeland.

But how does this impact your life? Let's get practical and let me share with you how to walk in financial integrity based on what the Bible teaches.

HOW TO WALK IN FINANCIAL INTEGRITY

1. Avoid the love of money.

The Bible teaches that the love of money is the root of all evil. The Bible doesn't say that money is the root of all evil, but the *love* of money. Jesus said you can't serve God and money. So ask your-self, "Is money and materialism a major issue in my life?" If you had asked me twenty years ago if money was an issue in my life, I would have told you "absolutely not." But then I went to Toronto in October that same year, and there God dealt with me about my love of money. Here is my testimony of how He convicted me, previously shared in my book *The Grace of Giving*:

Materialism Unmasked in My Life

The first time I stepped foot into Toronto Airport Christian Fellowship, the Lord convicted me of materialism. I was attending their first Catch the Fire Conference in the fall of 1994. On the second day of the conference, Mike Bickle, the founder of the International House of Prayer, was speaking at the morning session. He declared that we were engaging in idolatry if we were drawing life and security from anything other than Jesus. He ended by inviting the Holy Spirit to reveal to us if we had given our heart to something else besides the Lord. After he led us in a prayer, we were all dismissed for lunch.

While the other conference-goers made their way out of the room, I stayed in my seat and asked the Holy Spirit if I was finding security in anything other than Jesus. Right away, I heard a still, small voice say, "Son, you have a stronghold of materialism." I instantly rebuked the voice, completely disagreeing with what it said. In my mind, that voice couldn't have possibly been the real Holy Spirit. After all, we had just started HRock Church, and I went through the first five months of ministry there without receiving a salary. My wife, Sue, and I had continued to live by faith for nearly a year and a half now. Those actions certainly couldn't belong to a materialistic person!

But then the Holy Spirit spoke to me a second time: "I want to show you how strong this is in your life. I want you to take your retirement money and sow it into My kingdom." Sue and I had spent most of our savings to meet the cost of living, but we had accumulated a little more than $20,000 in our retirement account. When I heard God say this, my immediate response was "No, Lord!" (Of course, that reply is the ultimate oxymoron. How can you call Jesus "Lord" and say "no"? But that's what I said.) And as those words left my mouth, the realization swept me of how true God is and how much the stronghold of materialism had kept me bound in life. I wept for the next two hours. Some of those tears came because I still didn't want to give up my retirement money, but for the most part I was weeping honestly over my sins.

Finally, after two hours I realized that God wasn't planning on changing His mind, so I said, "OK, God. But this is not just my retirement money; it belongs to Sue, too. I have to call Sue and see if she will agree." (To this day, Sue and I wait to make any purchases, transactions, or gifts of more than $500 to any ministry until we first pray and talk to each other.) Quite frankly, I was relieved. Sue was back home in Pasadena, so this would be a cold call. She would be surprised and would never agree to the idea, and I'd be off the hook!

So I gave her a call. After I told Sue what I had sensed the Lord say, she paused to pray for a few moments. Then she replied, "That is the word of the Lord. Let's do it!" I couldn't believe it. Here I was in the midst of a revival in Toronto, and there she was 3,000 miles away. I spent two hours in a river of tears to reach the point of saying yes. She simply said yes in less than two minutes of praying! But, you see, this was not her problem. It was mine.

We weren't aware of it then, but God was testing our hearts, for in the future He was going to let us manage millions in the different ministries in which He called us to serve. This moment offered us another opportunity to train for reigning in His kingdom.

2. Faithfully support the church/ministry with your giving.

In His boundless wisdom, God has called His people to demonstrate love by the act of giving. Abba God loved us so much that He gave us His only begotten Son, but even beyond that, Jesus willingly gave of Himself. So, when we give with love as our motivation, we become like Christ. In Ephesians 5:1–2, the apostle Paul writes, *"Therefore be imitators of God, as beloved children; and walk in love, just as Christ also loved you and **gave** Himself up for us, an offering and a sacrifice to God as a fragrant aroma"* (NASB). Now, I personally believe that a good starting point for giving is to offer the first 10 percent of your gross income to the Lord. I can't remember the last time my wife and I didn't give at least 20 percent of our income. Not out of obligation, but because we wanted to. Then, after I heard Peter Wagner share how he and his wife, Doris, gave 40 percent of their income, Sue and I were inspired and decided to give the same ratio. In 2004, the Lord inspired us again to practice graduated giving: we set a goal to give more than 50 percent. We reached that goal in 2011, and ever since then we've been giving more than half of our income. Last year we ended up giving away 57 percent.

Why am I sharing this with you? Certainly not to make you feel guilty or ashamed if you're not matching the amount that Sue and I give! Something crucial I want to emphasize here is that you can't out-give God. During this season of giving between 40 and 50 percent, we were able to send our children to college without a trace of debt. My daughter Mary received her master's in public policy at Pepperdine (one of the more expensive private Christian universities), and we were able to buy three houses in the L.A. market. You simply can't out-give God! Another point I want to make clear is that you have to let the Holy Spirit lead you and be motivated to give by grace and love. That's the way we see believers giving in the New Testament. The principle boils down to the reality that you, too, can hear God and follow Him in faith as you begin practicing generosity. When we yield to the guidance of the

Spirit and give to advance His kingdom, the return on that investment becomes greater than any stock portfolio. I promise you that!

3. If in debt, deal with the root issue.

Most people today would agree with the statement that we have a money problem in America. What they might not realize is that the problem began long before the Great Recession of 2008. In 2003, a Gallup poll reported that 64 percent of American couples argued over money. Finances are now the number one cause of divorce—Americans vow to love "till debt do us part," as it were. It's estimated that more than 54 percent of divorces arise from conflicts over money issues.[21]

However, our money problem doesn't stop there. Consumer debt currently looms at $3.5 trillion in America.[22] I'm not talking about our national debt; that's our personal debt! This amount equals more than 150 percent of Russia's yearly gross national product. Although we live in the richest nation in the world, so many of us struggle with personal finances. I would like to propose to you that money isn't our problem. What do I mean by that? Let me explain.

Imagine you're at my house and you see me with a pair of garden shears in the backyard. As you walk up to me, you notice I'm cutting off stalks and leaves from a gigantic weed dominating my garden. You ask, "Ché, what are you doing?"

I immediately reply, "I'm pruning back these stalks and leaves because they get overgrown from time to time." What would you think? You'd think I was the worst gardener in the world! Of course, I could prune back the weed, but you know it would only reappear in the same spot because I'm completely ignoring the

---

21. Bruce Fleet, *Demystifying Wall Street* (Bloomington, IN: AuthorHouse, 2009), 151.

22. Martin Crutsinger, Associated Press, "Consumer credit up a record $28.9 billion in September," *Seattle Times*, November 6, 2015, http://www.seattletimes.com/business/us-consumer-credit-up-a-record-28-9-billion-in-september/ (accessed January 6, 2016).

roots. I can only get rid of the weed by attacking the roots and removing them.

I want to submit to you that our money problems do not just come from fiscal management difficulties or lack of knowledge, but issues in our heart. We could focus on budgeting and debt-reduction strategies, but those things won't give us lasting results. We're just lopping off the leaves of the weed without touching the root issue in our hearts. Our difficulty with money is a spiritual issue. If we don't trust our Abba God to provide for us—if we build without that solid foundation—we cannot truly prosper.

Several years ago, I met a woman who had worked as a top financial planner and earned a six-figure salary, counseling exclusive clients. I found out her personal finances were in shambles. Why? Despite all of her know-how and expertise, she unfortunately also had character issues deeply rooted within her heart that needed to be healed. She certainly wasn't committing a crime, like pastors who embezzle from their churches, but her distress came from the same place: the heart.

AN AFFAIR OF THE HEART

You see, our souls are the battlefield for our thoughts and feelings to wage war against each other. Logic tells us to do one thing, but our emotions sweep us away and lead us to behave irrationally. We repeatedly make resolutions to change our life for the better, but we only wind up in our same old lifestyle. Does this sound familiar? Unfortunately, this continual battle deeply discourages many Christians. In order to conquer the old habits that have too often kept us bound, we need to realize that we're not battling inside a vacuum. There are forces that come against us, called strongholds, and they often arise out of our hearts.

Our heart, also known as our reflective consciousness, is the seat of our personality. Our heart is the part of us that imagines, perceives, feels, reflects, desires, and wills. When we identify ourselves and say "I," we're referring to our heart. In both the Old and New Testaments, Scripture interchangeably translates the word "heart" as "spirit" or "soul." Actually, the heart is influenced by both the spirit and the soul, and it's the place where internal warfare rages. The battle is for our heart.

When our spirit is reborn in Christ, the Holy Spirit gives us access to the revelation of God's wisdom, but our soul still exerts its influence based on what we know and understand. For many of us, our heart bears deep wounds that we carry with us from experiences in our childhood or moments of trauma. Sometimes these negative circumstances can arise from an environment of abuse or neglect, but other times they can result from growing up in impoverished conditions, being an ethnic minority, being bullied by peers or other reasons. These types of experiences only add to the distortion in our understanding of our identity, our expectations of others and our overall lifestyle. As time goes by, we let these distorted ideas take root in our beliefs, and we re-create and perpetuate the things we believe. Proverbs 23:7 puts it this way: "As [a man] *thinks in his heart, so is he.*"

Distorted thinking creates habitual ruts in our lives. When we believe them for so long, the distortions seem like reality to us, trapping us in the lie that we can't choose different patterns of thought or behavior. Paul defines these habitual patterns as "strongholds." (See 2 Corinthians 10:3–5.)

In simple terms, a stronghold is a belief system consisting of certain thoughts, feelings, and behaviors. When a stronghold finds a place in our heart, it begins to filter reality and only let in the information that is in agreement with the stronghold. For example, if you dealt with a lot of disappointment as a child and a stronghold of mistrust developed, you most likely will find yourself doubting the motives of everyone around you. Receiving good things from others, including God, will be hard for you because the stronghold of mistrust feeds you with beliefs like "Nothing good ever happens to me." Therefore, even when your circumstances look good, you're convinced they can't be and your heart remains closed and unable to receive the good thing before you. And if you can't receive, you have nothing to give! Instead, you clutch greedily at what you think is "yours," like a little kid who holds on to her dirty, stinky, battered teddy bear while staring a giant room full of every kind of toy and book and stuffed animal purchased for her by a kind and loving dad.

SATAN'S STRONGHOLDS

While painful experiences can establish strongholds in our heart, we have to also be aware of other sources of strongholds that can work against us in powerful ways. One of these is the culture or worldview of the family and society that we belong to. We constantly hear messages from our parents, peers, teachers, media, movies, advertisements, etc., declaring that particular behaviors, values, aspirations, and ways of thinking are desirable or "right."

A few examples of the way American culture can influence and form strongholds in us include the craving to accumulate material possessions, the allure of fame, the desire for power, the value of science as a superior type of knowledge surpassing all others...I think you get the picture. All of these cultural influences are summed up in Paul's words as *"the wisdom of this world"*—something that he makes clear is foolishness to God. *"Let no one deceive himself. If anyone among you seems to be wise in this age, let him become a fool that he may become wise. For the wisdom of this world is foolishness with God"* (1 Corinthians 3:18–19).

We're also standing against a real adversary, Satan, who tries to steal from us, kill us, and destroy us. (See John 10:10.) The enemy likes to strategize and weaken our heart by accusing us. He can do this by setting up strongholds of self-condemnation, like shame, unworthiness, and guilt. Other strongholds try to appear as something praiseworthy, such as self-reliance or performance bent on gaining approval. All of these strongholds form barricades that try to deter us from trusting God's promises and fulfilling His purpose for our lives. They keep us clutching and controlling the miserable things of our life, spurning the gracious gifts of God.

Paul warns us in Ephesians 2:3:

> We as well as you once lived and conducted ourselves in the passions of our flesh [our behavior governed by our corrupt and sensual nature], obeying the impulses of the flesh and the thoughts of the mind [our cravings dictated by our senses and our dark imaginings].   (AMP)

Our old ways die hard, but Abba God has always given us the opportunity to choose life or death, blessing or cursing. (See Deuteronomy 30:19–20.) We have the responsibility to decide that we'll follow God's way, no matter how intense the battle becomes. We hear the message of wisdom: "Keep and guard your heart with all vigilance and above all that you guard, for out of it flow the springs of life" (Proverbs 4:23 AMP).

The good news is that we're not fighting alone. Abba God has given us the gift of His Holy Spirit, who has set us free from every form of curse and condemnation. (See Romans 8:1–2.) He has equipped us to overthrow every stronghold in our heart as we walk in our inheritance as God's children. Before we can gain victory over these areas, we must honestly look at our hearts and identify the strongholds we find there. We must focus on the condition of our heart first because it determines everything else in our life, including our financial integrity. We must open our heart for God's grace to transform us and make us more like Him. That's how we can become Christlike givers.

CATCHING HIS VISION

God originally fashioned us to function as a unified whole—spirit, soul, and body—with purpose and direction arising from our spirit. When strongholds are operating in our hearts, it become harder and harder to live with that purpose and direction. But just as the Father has overflowed our lives with so much good, we are able to break our strongholds and instead of clinging to areas of control, give freely—even crazily!—of our time, our money, and even our lives.

When it comes to giving, we give simply because our heavenly Father gave first. (See 1 John 4:19.) We're like a waterfall: constantly receiving from Him and pouring out to others. Dealing with money is, at its root, a heart issue, and we'll only maintain financial integrity through first attaining a giving heart. Jesus said He only did what He saw His Father doing, and we're meant to live—and give—in the same way. Abba God wants us to catch His vision of being a generous giver. That is the only path to financial integrity.

EIGHT

CINDY JACOBS

Integrity and Its Power of Moral Authority

Cindy Jacobs is a respected prophet who travels the world ministering not only to crowds of people, but also to heads of nations. Ever since the Lord called her with the Scripture, "Ask me, and I will make the nations your inheritance, the ends of the earth your possession" (Psalm 2:8 NIV), *she has taken that calling seriously. She has spoken on nearly every inhabited continent to tens of thousands. Yet, in her heart is the memory that Jesus left the ninety-nine to go to the one. Today, in spite of a demanding schedule, she is willing to go for the one lost soul. Cindy is the cofounder, along with her husband, Mike, of Generals International, formerly known as Generals of Intercession. Among other things, she is listed in the Who's Who Among American Women and has written for such publications as* Charisma, Ministries Today, *and* SpiritLed Woman. *Cindy has authored seven books:* Possessing the Gates of the Enemy, The Voice of God, Women of Destiny, Deliver Us from Evil, The Supernatural Life, The Reformation Manifesto, *and her newest,* The Power of Persistent Prayer. *Cindy and Mike have been married for forty-two years and reside in Dallas, Texas. They have two children and six grandchildren.*

Who you are is how you live your life when no one sees.
–Albert S. Johnson (My dad)

One summer when I was around eighteen years old, my family went to see a movie together. Just that, by itself, was unusual, since we didn't have an enormous amount of discretionary funds to make such a collective field trip. But it wasn't the most unusual part of our movie experience that night.

We all got settled into the movie atmosphere and the fun began! The plot pulled us in, and we were all enjoying the film until—all of a sudden, it seemed—the romantic interests who weren't married were taking a shower together. Even though "nothing showed" my dad stood up and whispered to us, "*We're leaving!*" At that point, without protest, to my recall, the whole family stood up and trooped out of the theater.

I confess, I was embarrassed! I don't know why, in looking back, because it was dark in the building and the place was practically empty. Not only did we leave, but, after we got our money refunded, my father respectfully told the attendants why he left. Then, he bought us tickets to another movie without questionable content that we all thoroughly enjoyed!

My daddy left a mark upon his children that day. He, a minister of the gospel, practiced what he preached. He had drawn a line in the sand for his family and said by his actions, "What you saw on the screen that day was wrong and we won't participate in sanctioning it by watching it or paying to see it." My dad always operated from the character and respectability he had obtained through righteous living, both publicly and privately. He was a man of strong moral authority. He could stand in the pulpit and preach with compassion and not condemnation that we must "be holy as He is holy." (See 1 Peter 1:16.)

Now, after he has been in heaven for forty-one years, I still respect him for that decision. The Holy Spirit still convicts me through that snapshot from our family's memory. There are times I have crossed that line and thought, "Well, I didn't see anything," only to later be struck in my heart by what I had done, and see a huge need to repent.

COUNTERCULTURAL IMPACT

Is this reaction extreme? No. Is it countercultural? Yes, *absolutely*! I realize that you may have a different opinion and have drawn different lines as to what you consider moral and immoral—the particulars you will have to wrestle out with God. But the principle remains: we must be countercultural.

I believe with all my heart that God is looking for a countercultural generation that is radically different from the world, without being judgmental in attitude.

Moral authority does not change because truth does not change. The principles of moral authority are immutable, or unchangeable. They are considered normative for behavior regardless of whether or not they are embodied in written laws and even if the community is ignoring or violating them.[23] Thus, moral authority can also be defined as the "fundamental assumptions that guide our perceptions of the world."[24]

Of course, the plumb lines for believers are the moral absolutes written in the Word of God! In other words, there are things that do not come in shades of gray but are either black or white; right or wrong.

As I am writing this, I am recalling a meeting of youth leaders in Mar del Plata, Argentina. The place was packed with passionate, "take the world for Jesus"-infused, next generation leaders— one of my favorite audiences! I love them because they are with you every moment. One only has to throw out a God-breathed challenge, and they jump on it with enthusiasm.

My topic for the day was "Ten Commandments, Not Ten Suggestions." As I taught, I told them God meant the "not" part. He wasn't merely suggesting that we not get into sexual sin—He meant it as a command. After I discussed problems with porn and sexual immorality in a loving but "thou shall not" way, many in the crowd, both young men and women, wept at the front as they repented and received healing prayers. (Of course, this is not meant to point a finger at a particular generation because sexual infidelity has no age limit.)

In an age of cultural relativism where there are not moral absolutes, this can be difficult for every generation. We are affected by the spirit of the age. One only has to read *Relevant* magazine and note that they have articles entitled "The Secret Sexual Revolution"[25] to see that the values from the "Summer of Love" in

23. Richard Norris and Timothy F. Sedgwick (editor), *The Business of All Believers: Reflections on Leadership* (New York: Church Publishing, Inc., 2009), 86.
24. James Davison Hunter, *Culture Wars* (New York: Basic Books, 1992), 119.
25. See article from the February 20, 2012 online issue, adapted from the September/October 2011 issue of *Relevant* magazine.

1967 in the San Francisco area have jumped the secular boundary and infiltrated the church.[26]

While the actual statistics of Christian young people having sex outside of marriage vary according to your source, every one is too high! A common thread to the articles about this issue is the compelling question, *What ever happened to abstinence?* While the polls are telling us that more and more people in America, and other nations as well, are against the murder of unborn children, still these abortions continue. Surely this demonstrates at least one root problem: as long as we as a culture continue to condone a hook-up mentality, women will continue to become pregnant outside the stability of a committed relationship—increasing the likelihood of an abortion. And why do Christians slide along with this cultural trend? Because we're abandoning our foundational moral absolutes that give us the moral authority to be countercultural.

But moral authority isn't just exhibited in hot-button cultural issues. Rather, it shows itself most clearly by a life of biblical integrity on all levels. Moral authority begins at the smallest of levels—like the movie theater—and then grows to apply to every part of our lives and our culture. To paraphrase the statement by my daddy, Rev. Albert S. Johnson, the way you obey God's Word when no one sees (except for God) is what you really believe. We might say we respect life and oppose abortion, but how often have we had hateful thoughts toward somebody else—disrespecting their lives! (See 1 John 3:15.) That's not integrity, it's hypocrisy.

IT'S THE TRUTH THAT SETS US FREE

One day my children and I ran into a little convenience store to buy something to drink. To my recollection, the children were around six and eight years old. After we made our purchase, I noticed we had been given a few cents too much change. I said to

26. The "Summer of Love" was a movement of around 100,000 hippies in which free food, free drugs, and "free love" were available in Golden Gate Park.

the kids, "We have to go back inside because the man gave me too much change."

When we went back to the cashier and handed him two pennies he looked very surprised. Why did I do that? Because a principle is a principle whether it is two pennies or two million dollars. One of the Ten Commandments forbids stealing. (See Exodus 20:14.) Simply put, stealing is taking what is not yours, no matter how small the amount—period! And so we gave the pennies back.

One thing that I admire about my husband, Mike (among many other things, I might add!), is his moral integrity. Years ago he worked at an airline as a financial comptroller. One day we got into a conversation about how people treat the companies where they are employed. "For instance," he shared, "they think nothing of taking pens or other office supplies home from the office." The fact that this problem bothered him touched my heart. Some people might think, *What is one little pen to a company that size?* But as a person who helps pay the bills for a large ministry, I can answer that because I think in these terms: "If one pen costs the company two dollars, hundreds of employees taking one pen runs up thousands of dollars in cost." Moral integrity, even on the smallest of issues, saves money for others—and it matters. These are the seemingly insignificant matters that the Scriptures call "*the little foxes that spoil the vines*" (Song of Solomon 2:15).

People often joke that evangelists have the gift of exaggeration. I know I have that gift! Especially when we evangelists speak about supernatural experiences, it is important that we state the facts rather than fabricate. Because evangelists, in some cases, can be rather flamboyant people, this can be harder than it would seem. But where does this tendency to exaggerate come from? Again, it stems from a lack of moral absolutes that weaken our ability to exercise moral authority in a countercultural way. Instead of taking the commandment "*You shall not bear false witness against your neighbor*" (Exodus 20:16) at its face value, as a moral absolute, we insert little qualifiers. The culture tells us that it's OK to tell a "little white lie," so we go along with it.

In God's eyes, however, there is no such thing as a white lie. There is only either the truth or the non-truth. This doesn't mean that there is never a time when we cannot be discreet or diplomatic, or that we should become more and more adept at soft answers that turn away wrath. (See Proverbs 15:1.) But we must be faithful in living our lives with the moral authority to say "no" to things that cross the line. I have personally had to go back to people to clarify my statements when I have crossed the line into white lies. And believe me, despite the discomfort or embarrassment, it's always worth it. The Word of God tells us that it is the truth that sets us free. (See John 8:32.)

A LONGING FOR INTEGRITY

I believe that the world is longing to believe that we, as believers, can actually "walk the walk" that God's Word lays out for us. There are times when I have watched the church being mocked for our failures by some comedian, and I have grieved for how we've fallen from a faithful city on a hill to a group of people who have little idea how to act with moral authority. Whether or not the culture believes, they are still watching, and, at moments, hoping that what we are saying is really true.

It is my dream that the next generation will be a bright light of holiness that our critics can admire rather than mock for our callous and hypocritical lives. There is, I believe with all my heart, a new holiness movement fueled by passionate young followers of the Way who will garner such respect as our Savior commanded from those around Him—who will live by moral absolutes to be salt and light in a tasteless, dark, cynical society. I believe we can gain the moral authority that gives us the right to speak against injustice and for the validity of God's laws. And not only do I long for this to be so, but my heart sees it on the horizon.

NINE

ALLEN HOOD

Integrity, Dominion, and the Family

Allen and Rachel Hood are full-time intercessory missionaries with the International House of Prayer in Kansas City,
Missouri, (IHOPKC), an evangelical missions organization
that is committed to praying night and day for the release of
the fullness of God's power and purpose as it actively wins the

lost, heals the sick, feeds the poor, makes disciples, and impacts every sphere of society. As associate director of IHOPKC, Allen leads one thousand full-time intercessory missionaries in helping to establish night and day prayer in every tribe and tongue. As president of the International House of Prayer University, he works to equip and send out missionaries as dedicated intercessors, evangelists, teachers, and pastors who will work to see revival within the church and a harvest among those searching for God. Allen and Rachel have three sons: Samuel, Jonathan, and Joshua.

The subject of dominion is a hot topic these days, and rightly so, for the dominion mandate given in the garden of Eden has not changed: *"Be fruitful and multiply; fill the earth and subdue it; have dominion over the fish of the sea, over the birds of the air, and over every living thing that moves on the earth"* (Genesis 1:28). Human beings made in the image of God were created to manifest God's kingdom rule in every arena of life.

Genesis 3 reveals the tragic moment when humanity entered the rebellion of Satan. Somewhere between Genesis 1:31, when God saw that all things were good, and Genesis 3, a conflict began in heaven. Tradition holds that Satan, a powerful and high-ranking angel, became proud of his angelic grandeur and exalted himself to be like God. (See Isaiah 14:14.) He sought the worship of God's created order and secured the following of a third of heaven's angels. (See Revelation 12:4.)

The rebellion extended to earth as Satan established his kingdom in the natural realm by seducing God's most prized creatures. Adam and Eve's decision to disobey God was about much more than which fruit to eat. Their decision was about whom humanity would listen to and follow: God or Satan. Humanity joined the resistance against God's plan, and the consequences of this rebellion have changed the entire landscape of the created order. The effects have been disastrous and deadly.

Humanity, in following Satan, fell from God's kingdom, and physical, spiritual, and eternal death entered into the human experience. The kingdom of darkness now has a stronghold on the earth, as the kingdoms of this world would come under Satan's rule. The Bible calls Satan the god of this age (see 2 Corinthians 4:4) and prince of the ruler of the air (Ephesians 2:2) and testifies that the entire world lies under the sway of the wicked one.

> *Again, the devil took Him up on an exceedingly high mountain, and **showed Him all the kingdoms of the world and their glory.** And he said to Him, "All these things I will give You if You will fall down and worship me."*
>
> (Matthew 4:8–9)

> *We know that we are of God, and **the whole world lies under the sway of the wicked one.***   (1 John 5:19)

The good news of the gospel is that God has a plan to restore all things. In the Person of Jesus Christ, God has removed the one weapon in Satan's arsenal against humanity: unforgiven sin. Now through the death of Christ on the cross, humanity can enter back into God's kingdom and manifest God's rule on this earth.

The victory over Satan, death, and sin has been secured by the atoning sacrifice, resurrection, and ascension of Christ Jesus, and will be consummated at His return. God has a plan to restore all things through the Person of His Son and disciple all nations through His redeemed, beloved people, who are washed by Christ's blood and filled with His Spirit.

GOD'S STRATEGY FOR RESTORATION

Malachi 4:5–6 reveals a key strategy in God the Father's end-time plan of restoration:

> *Behold, I will send you Elijah the prophet before the coming*
> *of the great and dreadful day of the LORD. And he will turn*
> *the hearts of the fathers to the children, and the hearts of the*
> *children to their fathers, lest I come and strike the earth with*
> *a curse.*   (Malachi 4:5–6)

What is astounding about this plan is not what it includes but what it excludes. God the Father's end-time plan does not center on governmental, religious, educational, business, or media institutions. Rather, the center of God's restoration plan focuses on the foundational reality of the family. God has ordained heavenly resources to turn the hearts of fathers to their children and the hearts of children to their fathers.

Why the emphasis on the family? There are two primary reasons. First, because God is a heavenly Father, and the heart of the gospel is a heavenly Father who wants a family and a heavenly Bridegroom who wants a bride. God is a family man and is by nature a Father! One of the Messiah's main titles in Isaiah 9:6 is *"Everlasting Father."* Jesus did not merely act like a father; His very name and nature is one of an everlasting Father. In John 17:25–26, Jesus defined His entire ministry as revealing His Father.

Second, because God entrusted the dominion mandate to Adam and Eve as a family unit, they were to subdue the earth for God through godly offspring. (See Genesis 1:26–28.) The family was the very place where the dominion mandate was given. In fact, the promise given to Abraham was that all the families of the earth would be blessed through him. (See Genesis 12:3.) There is no power on earth greater than a family filled with the power and presence of the living God walking in the unity of the Spirit, full of integrity before themselves and the world.

The evil one has assaulted the very basis of the dominion mandate by attacking the family structure. From the beginning, Satan has worked to sow discord in marriages and turn brother against brother. The enemy is an expert at causing fathers and children to turn away from each other. And America, as a whole and including the church, is currently feeling the disastrous effect of this warfare. The 2010 US Census has revealed disturbing trends in our nation.

America had 74.7 million children under the age of eighteen in 2010. Approximately 27 percent of children (19.8 million) lived with only one parent, in most instances their mother (23 percent of all children lived with their mother but not fathers). Ten percent of children living with two parents (5.3 million) lived with a biological parent and a step-parent. Most of these children (4.1 million) lived with their mother and a stepfather. One in ten children lived in their grandparents' home. These shocking statistics caused the current administration to remedially initiate in 2011 a "Year of Strong Fathers, Strong Families."

The National Fatherhood Initiative exhorts: "Right now, there are 24 million children living in a home without their biological father. These children are more likely to live in poverty, drop out of school, engage in risky behaviors, and suffer from emotional and behavioral issues."[27]

But alongside these disheartening statistics, we have Malachi's promise that the Spirit will work in the church to turn the hearts of the fathers to the children and the hearts of the children to their fathers. God has an answer to the crisis: it is the spirit and power of Elijah resting upon the Christian home.

THE ROLE OF A FATHER

The Lord is restoring fatherhood as the foundation of mature ministry. What does fatherhood have to do with integrity? Well, men are meant, designed, and called to be fathers, and it is only when they are loyal to the truth of their identity, when they live in integrity as who they were meant to be, that the church will triumph over the powers of hell. The restoration of fatherhood, of

---

27. See http://www.fatherhood.org.

manhood's call and purpose, is foundational to our victory. God will restore spiritual fathers (apostles, prophets, etc.) in the church, who will lead the church to maturity. (See Ephesians 4:11–13.) The apostles and prophets of our generation will be fully established as men filled with the heart and wisdom of a father. (See 1 Thessalonians 2:11; 1 Corinthians 4:14–15; 1 John 2:13–14.)

God will restore natural fathers to their natural children even in a generation filled with divorce, reconciling these hurting relationships. Before Christ's return, the Lord will establish men in a fathering role to children who are not even physically related to them, thus revealing His heart toward His people. It is supernatural for men to deeply care for other people's children—it takes integrity not just to their natural identity as fathers to their own children, but also integrity to their spiritual identity as fathers to all children.

The present movement of adoption is a supernatural activity of the Holy Spirit to restore the fathering heart back to the church. George Whitefield often stated that the greatest thing he accomplished in his life was the orphanage he began in Georgia. This is a staggering statement from one of our nation's greatest evangelists who preached the gospel before tens of thousands in the First Great Awakening. Despite his fame, despite the huge numbers he drew, he still thought caring for the fatherless was his most important work.

Some may not be able to adopt a child into their family, yet they may be able to take a step toward parenthood by adopting the kids on the block into their heart. I have made a commitment to help strengthen the kids on my block in the grace of God.

What men believe about their individual responsibility as fathers to their natural and spiritual children is one of the most significant issues to settle in seeking to expand the kingdom of God. Families without committed fathers, churches that permit their members to neglect the children (especially the children of single mothers), and ministries lacking a father's heart and wisdom are extremely ineffective in restoring the kingdom on earth as it is in heaven.

The dominion mandate entrusted to the church depends upon godly men cooperating with the Holy Spirit until a father's heart is fully established in them. God requires men (single, married, young, and old) to function as fathers in the house of God; He requires the enormous commitment of time and energy necessary to properly train children. Being graced by God with a father's wisdom and gentleness is one of the great privileges of men in this generation. (See Deuteronomy 6:6–7.)

CHILDREN ARE A BLESSING!

Psalm 127 gives powerful promises related to the family and portrays the family as God's chosen vessel for warfare. Most ministries focus on the members who have the greatest resources and who can increase and extend the ministry's influence. But they only focus on such outward manifestations of influence because they lack the foresight of understanding the long-term impact that investing in the children and youth will have on the city and nations. The family unit is a fully-engaged, independent, creative cell for the advancement of the kingdom. Psalm 127 gives biblical insight into this reality:

> Unless the LORD builds the house, they labor in vain who build it; unless the LORD guards the city, the watchman stays awake in vain. It is vain for you to rise up early, to sit up late, to eat the bread of sorrows; for so He gives His beloved sleep.
>
> (Psalm 127:1–2)

God is committed to building our houses and calls us to believe in Him and resist anxiety. We must build our families in faith instead of the fear of the future that can drive us to anxiously overwork. God promises to intervene as we build our homes, and therefore it is presumptuous to underwork and vain to overwork in this area. God will give us wisdom if we ask Him. (See James 1:5.) If we do our simple part of obedience, the Lord will do His larger part. We must walk in faith, praying and believing God's promises, including this one: *"Children are a heritage from the LORD, the fruit of the womb is a reward"* (Psalm 127:3).

The trend today is to see children as interrupting our careers and our time for leisure and recreation. Many people wrongly choose career, money, a bigger house, and more free time over having more children. Such an attitude, although it may appear wise, deceptively distracts us from living in integrity according to our true identity. My wife, Rachel, challenged me in this very area when we were newly married, without children.

I was delivering pizzas to pay my way through graduate school. There was little free time, and we were barely making it. My wife raised the issue of us having children. I quickly refuted the idea, saying, "It's not time to have children. We have to survive. I've got to finish graduate school. We have to get our feet financially grounded."

She suggested, "Allen, it's not a financial issue; you are just afraid. Besides, I don't believe you have God's heart for children. Why don't you do a Bible study on how God feels about children and come back and give me a report?"

Over the next week I did the study and was undone by what I found. She was right. I did not have the Lord's heart for children. I asked God to forgive me for my low view of children—presented in God's Word as one of His most precious gifts! Part of our identity is caring for children, whether ours or another's! Rachel and I knelt down by our bed, and I repented before the Lord for my wrong attitude, committing my trust fully to Him. A month later she was pregnant with our first child, Samuel.

God desires that we would see all children that He entrusts as gifts and rewards. God didn't interrupt your good life to give you a child; He gave you a child to bless your life, to give you the deeper things of the kingdom like humility, patience, and meekness. This is a spiritual revelation. God has temporarily entrusted children to us as individual families and as a church body. We are our brother's keeper (see Genesis 4:9); therefore, together we bear the concern for all the children given to us as a church. Our children's ministry is our joint responsibility. It is a privilege because God has given us a multitude of children as a reward and gift for our faithfulness to Him.

Like arrows in the hand of a warrior, so are the children of one's youth. Happy is the man who has his quiver full of them; they shall not be ashamed, but shall speak with their enemies in the gate.   (Psalm 127:4–5)

Our children are like arrows in the hand of the Lord. In the psalmist's day, each arrow was individually made by the warrior who used it. We must see each child's unique potential according to God's purpose. Each child entrusted to us must be individually cared for, loved, and trained in order to fulfill their special God-given role in the future battle.

Let me develop this a bit. There is a serious battle going on right now and a serious enemy on the other side. God has given His army powerful weapons called arrows. The arrows are our children, individually and corporately, who are being prepared to minister God's grace to the nations. These arrows are the young apostles, prophets, teachers, evangelists, pastors, elders, deacons, scientists, doctors, lawyers, media messengers, songwriters, business leaders, and entrepreneurs being prepared for tomorrow. Do you know what God made them for and how He brought them forth to combat a certain work of darkness through their talents and gifts?

Today, I have three teenage sons. We are contending with our enemies at the gate—pornography, lust, anger, fear, pride, lethargy, and compromise. They are not merely a pastor's children. They have been born into an epic war between light and darkness, good and evil. I am their father in this battle, and even greater, they are my brothers in Christ, especially made to resist the works of darkness as a family and bring Christ's kingdom to our world.

I remember when the Holy Spirit gave me a word of knowledge concerning an area in which the evil one was trying to get a foothold in my son's life. I asked him, "Son, what have you been doing today?"

"Nothing," he replied.

I softly answered, "The reason I asked is that the Lord impressed upon me some things you were actually doing."

When I shared the impressions, he broke down weeping, fell into my arms and said, "Dad, I've been so scared to tell you, thinking you would be ashamed of me, thinking you would be so disappointed that I had fallen to these things."

And I quickly responded, "Son, I'm not ashamed of you, I just want an opportunity to fight this thing with you. We are in this together for life. You boys and I will be contending all our lives together for holiness and purity. You just need to know that we are in this together. One can put a thousand to flight but two can put ten thousand."

FIVE WAYS TO TURN OUR HEARTS TO OUR CHILDREN

Malachi 4:5–6 is often quoted but rarely discussed practically. What does it mean for a father to turn his heart to his children? Over the years the Lord has spoken to me on how I am to turn my heart toward my children in five specific ways. Because of the enormity of the crisis in the church right now, because of how many men are slacking while their wives fight to carry the load, men desperately need these words of truth, and so I'm writing directly now to Christian men to live before the Lord in integrity, although much of the following applies to women as well.

1. Ask the heavenly Father to reveal to us His loving, righteous heart.

Independent of how our fathers treated us, we must receive the love of our heavenly Father in our hearts and forgive and bless our earthly fathers. We are incredibly aware of our fathers' shortcomings and our own shortcomings that continue to manifest themselves in our relationships with our children. Why are we so aware? Because we are all craving a father's love—but only our Father in heaven can really fulfill it. And that's ok. If we are confident of His love, we can trust our earthly fathers as well.

At the beginning of Jesus' earthly ministry, the Father solidified Jesus' confidence in His identity. At the height of Jesus' earthly ministry, at the hour before the cross, the Father once again strengthened His Son with these same words. Jesus could trust the Father in the hour of the cross, because He was confident in His Father's love.

> And suddenly a voice came from heaven, saying, "This is My beloved Son, in whom I am well pleased."   (Matthew 3:17)

> While he was still speaking, behold, a bright cloud overshadowed them; and suddenly a voice came out of the cloud, saying, "This is My beloved Son, in whom I am well pleased. Hear Him!"   (Matthew 17:5)

It is easy for us to see God's affection and love for the Lord Jesus, yet it is difficult to believe these words to Jesus can transfer to us. The question becomes: can the Father feel toward us like He feels toward Jesus? The measure of the Father's love for Jesus is the measure of His love for us. This is the ultimate revelation of our worth. It gives every believer the right to view himself or herself as "God's favorite." John 17:23 says, "...*that the world may know that You...have loved them as You have loved Me.*"

The Father feels about you in the same way that He feels about Jesus. He will not increase in His love for Jesus, nor will He ever love anyone more than He loves Jesus. Therefore, since He loves you in the same way, He will never increase or decrease in the measure He loves you. Our faith in God's love does not change the measure of His love toward us. It simply changes the measure of our experience of His love. We love Him when we discover how vast His love is for us. "*We love Him because He first loved us*" (1 John 4:19). And again, "*As the Father loved me, I also have loved you*" (John 15:9).

We must ask the Holy Spirit to guide us into the truth about the Father loving us like He loves Jesus. The Holy Spirit is an indispensable aid to living in integrity, because only the Spirit can convict our hearts of the truth. The Holy Spirit has the same ministry focus as Jesus, to help us experience the Father. He cries out to God through us as the "*Spirit of adoption*" crying, "*Abba*" (Romans 8:15). Abba is a term of endearment like "Papa." It is respectful, yet affectionate and intimate. "*Now hope does not disappoint, because **the love of God has been poured out in our hearts by the Holy Spirit** who was given to us*" (Romans 5:5).

2. As fathers, we must ask the Lord to turn our hearts toward our children.

The Lord wants our hearts to turn. There is a required turning, and we must ask the Lord to give us His heart for our children. The Lord is inviting us into a season of prayer, reflection, repentance, and acts of love.

Many generations are willing to sell out their children's legacy for their own short-term gratification. For example, Hezekiah was willing for his descendants to experience invasion and exile as long as it did not happen personally to him:

> *"And they shall take away some of your sons who will descend from you, whom you will beget; and they shall be eunuchs in the palace of the king of Babylon." So Hezekiah said to Isaiah, "The word of the LORD which you have spoken is good!" For he said, "At least there will be peace and truth in my days."*
>
> (Isaiah 39:7–8)

Or again, David's adulterous affair with Bathsheba released destruction within his own house:

> *"Now therefore, the sword shall never depart from your house, because you have despised Me, and have taken the wife of Uriah the Hittite to be your wife." Thus says the LORD: "Behold, I will raise up adversity against you from your own house; and I will take your wives before your eyes and give them to your neighbor, and he shall lie with your wives in the sight of this sun. For you did it secretly, but I will do this thing before all Israel, before the sun."*   (2 Samuel 12:10–12)

As fathers we must ask the Lord to reveal to us the ways the enemy has caused us to subtly turn from our children due to contention, personality conflicts, or their continued resistance to our requests. By so doing, we have lived deceitfully before our children: ostensibly putting them first, but underneath seeking only our own gain.

In my teenage years I went through a season of rebellion where I was testing the waters and resisting my dad's clear boundaries. It was then that my father was faced with a decision. He could clamp down on me and force me from the home, or he could receive a supernatural love from heaven that would enable him to chase after me when I was truly undeserving of any kindness or mercy. My father chose to receive the heavenly Father's unmerited love and then turn his heart to me in a new way. Over the next year my father's love toward me broke through and turned my wayward heart back to the Lord.

One important way to turn our hearts to our children is by asking their forgiveness for our shortcomings on a regular basis. One of the most powerful gifts you can give your children is a transparent heart that is willing and quick to say, "I'm sorry." I often tell my sons, "Boys, there are many things that you will have to forgive your mom and me for just as your children will have to forgive you for many of your shortcomings. No matter how we have fallen short, you must forgive us, because whatever you do not forgive us for, you get to keep. There is only one way to keep our shortcomings from becoming yours—forgiveness!"

3. We must turn our hearts to our children by understanding the importance of building a family altar and recording our family's prophetic storyline.

Abraham walked the land and built altars of worship that attracted the presence of God to the land. In fact, throughout Genesis the children of Israel encountered God in the very locations where Abraham had built altars unto the Lord.

We want to build altars of worship in our homes that attract the presence of God and lead to encounters for our children. Isaac, Jacob, and Joseph had encounters and dreams in places where Abraham worshipped. You've heard it said that the marriage that prays together stays together. It is also true that the family that worships together stays together. Are you building altars of worship where your children and grandchildren can encounter God?

Encourage your children to write songs and to lead worship in the home setting, and practice call-and-response prayer and worship with them. Singing in your home is vital! There is no replacement for singing in establishing a positive spiritual atmosphere in your home. Don't be religious with your children! Just sing!

As a father, do you have a prophetic history, and are you forming a prophetic history with your family? Is your family tracing the beautiful storyline of God's redemptive hand? We are to foster a heart attitude that cultivates a prophetic, watchful spirit. Fathers are to hear what the Spirit is saying to the church. I've seen too many homes where the wife is prophetically sharp but the husband has a dull, lethargic spirit. This must change. We have no idea of the power of a father with a watchful spirit. Jonadab's spiritual alertness in Ahab's and Jezebel's day (see 2 Kings 10:15) reaped fruit two hundred and fifty years later in Jeremiah 35:

> And Jeremiah said to the house of the Rechabites, "Thus says the LORD of hosts, the God of Israel: 'Because you have obeyed the commandment of Jonadab your father, and kept all his precepts and done according to all that he commanded you, therefore thus says the LORD of hosts, the God of Israel: "Jonadab the son of Rechab shall not lack a man to stand before Me forever."'"   (Jeremiah 35:18–19)

4. As fathers, we must accept the primary responsibility of training and equipping our children in the ways of the Lord.

We are not to wait for a church program to reform our wayward children. Christian education is primarily a family responsibility. Early in my ministry, the Holy Spirit whispered something to me in my time of prayer that has changed the focus of my ministry: "Is it OK with you if I decide to fulfill the dreams that I have put in your heart through your three sons?" Suddenly, I knew that the success of my ministry would be measured through the success of my three sons.

Paul only gives two admonitions to fathers in the New Testament. He repeats the first one twice, exhorting fathers not to provoke their children to wrath. Fathers are tempted to enforce obedience through severity and displays of anger, but Paul warns that it shouldn't be so: "*And you, fathers, do not provoke your children to wrath, but bring them up in the training and admonition of the Lord"* (Ephesians 6:4). And again, *"Fathers, do not provoke your children, lest they become discouraged"* (Colossians 3:21).

One summer our family joined another family for a summer vacation in Wyoming and Montana. Shortly into the trip, my oldest son, who was twelve at the time, decided to be abnormally disobedient and obnoxious. It was especially embarrassing due to the fact that the other family was in ministry, too. Their kids were acting like angels, serving and complying. My oldest son was getting in fights, talking back, and being plain rude. The more my son disobeyed, the more I clamped down. For five days I laid into my kid.

On the night before returning home, I had a dream concerning an attack of witchcraft upon my oldest son. Suddenly, it dawned on me that my son was not usually like this. He was a responsible and respectful young man. It also dawned on me that my punishment of him was more due to the embarrassment it was causing me in front of the other family than due to how I would normally handle it.

While driving home, I began to pray for my son and ask the Lord to deliver us from all attacks of the enemy. What happened next deeply impacted me. After a time of prayer, my son began to cry uncontrollably and tell me over and over how sorry he was. He said, "Dad, I'm so sorry. Every night I would pray and ask God to help me obey, and every day I would wake up and do the very same thing. It felt like something was controlling me. I'm so sorry that I disappointed and embarrassed you and Mom." As fathers we must pray for our children and avoid harsh punishment—especially if we are punishing our child for embarrassing us rather than punishing them for disobeying the Lord!

Paul's second word of caution is for fathers to bring up their children in the training and admonition of the Lord. Paul declares that it is the father's responsibility to take on the spiritual development of his children and to do so in a spirit of humility and loving instruction, not in religious harshness.

As fathers we must reflect upon our children's designs and call them forth, giving them a vision for how God may use them. We must understand that our children are great weapons in the hand of the Lord, and we need to recognize the great battle raging to destroy our marriages and families. If we live in integrity before our children, they will carry that picture with them for the rest of their lives, and, in turn, live in integrity before their Lord. Our kids see us at our worst. They will see through our lies faster than anybody else. So be honest with them, even asking their forgiveness when appropriate.

We must teach our children how to pray and worship through relationship. Continually look for ways to call your children forth in nonreligious and unplanned settings. Holding high standards without including play and wonder in your relationship with your kids will cause your children to have a locked-up heart. You want your children to have an unlocked, flowing heart in God, where dialogue with you and with God is easy, playful, and sober when appropriate.

Embrace a missionary life versus a western, professional minister vocation. Missionary families do it together. Take your kids with you, not as a cute thing, but as an integral part of doing the Lord's will. Avoid the necessity of having everything fixed and in order all at once. There are seasons of sowing and seasons of reaping. Know which one you are in and be at peace. Remember the big picture, and let time do its good work.

5. We must turn our hearts to our children by maintaining an unwavering commitment to our wives.

The bloodiest and most violent battlefields in history were not those at Iwo Jima, Okinawa, or the Battle of the Bulge in World

War II. They are in our homes, our bedrooms, and our minds at work. We must commit to faithfulness in the marriage and home.

The responsibility for the building of a family altar begins with the husband's treatment of his wife. Everything hinges upon this. If the husband does not serve and cherish his wife, he will not have a spirit of prayer upon his life. This is why the prayer rooms of the earth are predominately made up of women. Without a spirit of prayer upon the man, the effectiveness of the family altar will be greatly reduced.

> *Husbands, likewise, dwell with them with understanding, giving honor to the wife, as to the weaker vessel, and as being heirs together of the grace of life, that your prayers may not be hindered.* (1 Peter 3:7)

Scripture calls us to understand and honor our wives as equal partners and heirs in the kingdom. Any man who fails to do this will be hindered in his prayer life. We must give her equal respect in the kingdom as co-heirs in the grace of God. Growing in prayer is linked to honoring and understanding women. The end-time prayer movement is a movement to honor marriage. As husbands, we are to commit to understand and honor our wives, regardless of how we feel about them romantically in a given season. We must get a vision for a godly heritage where the blessing of the Lord flows down upon our children and grandchildren. I have a great vision to grow old with my wife, Rachel, watching our grandchildren reap the blessings of a life fully and faithfully given to the ways of the Lord.

The center of God's restoration plan focuses on the foundational reality of the family. It is the true, integrity-filled calling of every man. Before the coming of the great and terrible day of the Lord, we have a powerful promise. The Holy Spirit will be working to turn the hearts of fathers to their children and the hearts of children to their fathers.

Father, send the spirit and power of Elijah to Your church again. Release Your great power to turn our hearts and bring spiritual revival to our families. Bring forth Your dominion through our families, bringing forth a godly heritage with fruit that remains. Amen.

TEN

CHARLES STOCK

Love: Integrity's Sure Foundation

Charles Stock has been stirring passionate people to follow Jesus to the ends of the earth for over thirty years. He carries joyful love and delights in breaking religious boxes and bringing believers into freedom! Senior leaders at Life Center in Harrisburg, Pennsylvania, Charles and Anne Stock have developed a community culture centered around the active *presence of the Holy Spirit, encounters with missional love, tangible joy, and radiant living.*

Let's change the world! Come on! Isn't that what every single one of us wants to do? Here's how to do it, in the words of a simple worship chorus I heard at a gathering of young revivalists:

First we're going to fall in love,
Then we're going to change the world!
Let's keep first things first.

One of the greatest historical failings of the worldwide body of Christ has been the ineffective witness of an extraordinary love for one another. There have been exceptions to that statement, but mostly the surrounding multitudes are not crying out in awe and wonder, "See how they love one another!"

It's not like we don't want to love one another, or even that we don't at times or even most of the time love one another. It's just that we do not **only always** love one another! That's the gold standard of heaven: Only Always Love.

This is the John 15 standard: *"As the Father has loved me, so have I loved you. Now remain in my love.... My command is this: Love each other as I have loved you"* (John 15:9, 12 NIV).

This is God's idea of relational integrity. It is true holiness and it is participation in the activity and nature of God! *"And so we know and rely on the love God has for us. God is love"* (1 John 4:16 NIV). Whoever lives in love lives in God, and God in him. Whoever lives in love, lives in God? And God lives in him? Let's stay in love! Only love, all the time. It fills us with joy and opens up miracles and provision.

HOW WE ENDED UP IN LOVE

Now that I've started off with a little "preach," let me introduce myself. My wife Anne and I met Jesus in 1972 and have been following Him and been serving in some kind of leadership continuously since 1975. It was never my ambition to be a minister or a leader, but I did want to obey Him, and He wanted me to serve in leadership.

For two long stretches of that time I have served on pastoral teams of local churches that had apostolic impact: training and sending out ministries, planting local churches, and pioneering creative approaches to fill the earth with the culture of heaven.

Early successes

For ten years I was part of an amazing church in California's Sierra Nevada Mountains. Out in the middle of nowhere, God poured out His presence and blessings and we saw year after year of growth and revival. The structure was somewhat unique and, in that season, creative and fruitful. There were three co-pastors, who related to each other with good humor, honor, and humility. In addition, we had a bunch of our friends who made up the elder board. We were mostly young "elders," in our twenties and thirties, but God poured out His blessing and the little chapel grew to around one thousand people in Sunday attendance, which made it a kind of megachurch out in the middle of the mountain forests. Despite its size, it was a loving and tight-knit community. It was a spiritual hot spot. People would drive an hour or two to experience the presence of God in the meetings.

Transition through the valley of the shadow

This "holy experiment" in a shared leadership did really well until the time came for a big change—my best friend became the senior pastor. That was totally fine with me, I had always seen it that way. But we needed to go away in order for him to clearly carry out his mission. The problem was that we were young and inexperienced, and none of us understood the unusual thing God was doing. It was a very painful time for us, and for our friends as well. For ten years Anne and I had sacrificially poured ourselves into every dimension of the ministry. We had seen so much good fruit, but this change was confusing and dangerously painful to our mental and physical health.

In all the confusion we remained sure of a few things: we didn't want to split the church and we didn't want to defile the wonderful people who simply loved Jesus and didn't have a clue what was going on in the inner circle of leadership. In the pain, we did our best to keep our mouths shut. We were loyal and didn't want to leave.

The more damaged we got, the more trapped we felt! It was a downward spiral. *"Help!"* we cried in our hearts, and God indeed sent prophets! A dear friend ours, Lonnie Frisbee, had a word for us, "Danger, danger! Run for your lives!" Another prophet encouraged us, "This is like Joseph and his brethren: you need to flee." A few others spoke into our lives, all saying the same thing in several different ways.

I want to make this very clear: the problem wasn't the other leaders, it was all of us, and mostly the toxic reaction that Anne and I were having to all the "adjustment" and the false beliefs that held us there longer than was healthy. In all our pain, a totally unlikely door opened up on the East Coast. God spoke clearly to me to go. Anne laid out a four-part "fleece": that our cute mountain home that I had built myself and was miraculously debt-free would sell the first day on the market, to the first person who looked at it, for the full price, and that the buyer would offer cash. I liked this, because I thought it could never happen and that I could then dismiss what I had heard as self-deception, quit the ministry, and go to work as a carpenter until I had gotten my emotional equilibrium back. But, it sold exactly according to the conditions Anne had prescribed. Ten days later we were in a rental truck with our car in tow, traveling, like Abraham and Sarah, to a land we had never seen.

This whole experience was a purifying fire for us and lasted about eighteen months. Yikes! It was horrible, dangerous, and in its fruit, totally worth it.

In my darkest times, I would break down weeping and declare, "Jesus, no matter how much I have been hurt or betrayed, I love You, and I love Your people! I'm not mad at anyone. I just want to be filled with Your love." That's the gold that came through the fire. We found love, which filled us with integrity, even amidst all the pain.

Other than the last painful year, we had a great adventure in California, pioneering worship, intercession, missions, and church planting. It was mostly wonderful for nine years. The year or so of unexpected suffering was a "boundary event," a real black hole that sucked us into and through a valley of the shadow of death. And on the other side was the table that the Lord prepared for us! He anointed our heads with oil and poured wine into our overflowing cups. We look back with a shudder of pain if we focus on the suffering, but mostly with profound gratitude that what didn't kill us made us much more resilient. This was all preparation for the next phase, which has lasted for over twenty-seven years. It was the set-up for what has been by far the most adventurous and fruitful years of our lives.

On the East Coast we have been key links in a chain of events that has made our new home base in Pennsylvania a hub of spiritual awakening and a center for training and sending ministers and missionaries all over the globe. We are spiritual parents to a multigenerational spiritual and creative community of wild, joyful lovers of God and man, full of unsinkable faith.

But all of this would have short-circuited if we hadn't made it through the tough times. The "keys" that unlock the doors of destiny and give believers love and integrity are really simple:

1. Our ambition was always to follow Jesus, never to have a title or position. That kept our hearts from retaliation, revenge, or trying

to "prove" that we were the anointed ones. We don't need a title to change the world; we just need great love! If we acquire something by self-effort, we will wear ourselves out trying to maintain it.

2. We forgave and forgave and forgave unconditionally, just because we knew we had to if we wanted to be healed. In my darkest pain, I discovered that total forgiveness is like an onion with many layers. I needed to repeatedly forgive some of the hurtful dynamics, because in weak moments the memories would stab my heart and tempt me to hold a grudge or live in anger. What seemed like betrayals or injustice would circle back and replay at unexpected times. Again and again I forgave, and in that I found healing, love, and joy. During this time, we were isolated, in culture shock, enduring a cold and lonely winter. Each time a thought or feeling would resurface, I would forgive again and again relentlessly until I felt love and affection for our friends who had been part of the pain.

Don't stop at a "truce." Go for restored friendship! The wonderful thing about unconditional forgiveness is that it is an act of royal generosity. Only kings can grant unconditional pardon. Each time we forgive, we enter the deep heart of God and the fellowship of His sufferings. Oh, that we might know Him!

3. We took full responsibility. No one actually has the power to ruin our lives, unless we give them that power by making ourselves victims. We sought help, not for our leadership skills but for our hearts. And we paid the bills for the help we sought. We didn't realize at the time that this was a huge investment for the future. When your heart is established in love, nothing is impossible!

So we made it through the dark and dangerous night of our soul with our love still intact and our sanity mostly restored. God is good!

A new day dawns

When we arrived in Pennsylvania in October 1987, I happened to meet the founding pastor of a dynamic young church.

Almost six months later we attended his church on a Sunday morning. The pastor asked me if I would like to preach, and I was put on the schedule for an evening service a couple weeks later. Preaching that evening, I was overtaken by a hilarious, cathartic joy. The pastor fell off his chair face down on the floor and stayed there! I had no idea why, but I just kept preaching.

The next day he took me to lunch and played a recording of a prophecy the church had received the previous year that stated *God would send a man who would play a key role in the ministry.* He believed I was the man. That was a surprise! We prayed and wondered if this could be part of the reason we had crossed the nation. We were encouraged but not sure. However the next Sunday he read the prophecy to the congregation and then said, "Charles Stock, stand up!" When I stood, he said, "This is the man!" He brought me to the front and laid hands on me! I didn't know what it all meant, but obviously God was at work. It was Father's Day, 1988.

A month later, I was given a small salary and a position as an associate pastor. This young pastor who hired me had established a small network of churches. He wanted to be freer to minister to them and to speak in other places, so I was a piece of the puzzle. The first few months were fun and without a lot of pressure. He was a brilliant teacher with great gifts of healing and faith. We were learning the ropes in a brand-new setting. But there was something more going on in his life. About two months after I came, he abruptly left the church and broke many hearts.

So there we were, newcomers and strangers in a strange land. I thought I had found a safe place for my family, and now the rug was pulled out from under my feet! One weekday morning I was at the church, praying alone in the sanctuary, deeply concerned for the church, the pastor who had left, and for all whose hearts were crushed.

I said something like, "Oh, God, this is really bad. I don't want people to harden their hearts, especially the children. Don't let them become cynical and lose their trust in You. If needed, I will stay here and help until they find a new pastor."

In my mind I wondered if we would move back to the West Coast. I was so surprised to hear the Lord speak clearly and say, "I have set you here." Shock!

I responded to God, "You will have to tell that to a lot of people, because I certainly won't make that announcement!" And, in God's good pleasure, after a few months, I was appointed as the new senior pastor.

This was a crazy turn of events! I would have never guessed it, and I didn't feel ready for this. But God's choice was clear. Almost from the first Sunday I would be overcome by a joyful vision of a youthful mission movement flowing out of the church. I would prepare what I thought would be a sensitive message to bring healing to hearts and instead I would spontaneously declare that revival was coming. It would well up in my heart as I spoke. It seemed crazy in the context of this church that was so disappointed, but it was heaven-sent, crazy, wild, *hope!*

Note well: *the reason you think you are in a place may not be the real reason!* He is faithful, but we often discover His purposes only after we've taken a few steps into the unknown. His plans are too wild for our tame thinking.

We didn't realize it, but as a family, we had stepped into a zone best described by Paul's outburst of praise, *"Now to him who is able to do immeasurably more than all we ask or imagine…"* (Ephesians 3:20 NIV). We were in the *"immeasurably more"* zone!

It didn't look that way. The cards were stacked against us. The church met in a big, dilapidated, ugly building in the worst part of town. We had to hire off-duty policemen so that cars wouldn't be stolen. There were drive-by shootings. The building had once been a casket warehouse and showroom, and it was long past even that auspicious heyday.

We faced suspicion and accusation from those who didn't know us. There was a small group of pastors from the network of churches who were hurt by the failure of the founding pastor. Some of them suspected me of being the culprit. We needed incredible love in order to continue.

Discovering the power of joy

One day two of these pastors came to see me. They brought along a prophet from Chicago for good measure. They thought I was unqualified for the role of senior pastor and advised that I vacate the corner office and the title immediately. The prophet really got going! He passionately warned me that if I stayed, this whole ministry would collapse within a year. He got so into it that he stood up, preaching right in my face.

I said in my heart, "Jesus, this is really hard. Help me!"

I heard the response, "Rejoice and be glad!" I instantly recognized the phrase from the Sermon on the Mount.

I raised my hand for a timeout. When the prophet paused, I said, "I remembered I need to do something. Be back in a couple minutes."

Leaving the office, I walked briskly to the far corner of the building and entered an isolated room. I closed the door and began to jump up and down shouting, "Thank You, Jesus! Thank You! This is so awesome! They are saying all kinds of bad things about me! Oh, thank You! Hallelujah!"

While I jumped and shouted, *I felt a big rush of joy wash over me.* It filled me with clarity and gratitude. Because I responded in spirit and in truth to the Spirit's prompting, He didn't let me down. I returned to the meeting, sat down, and asked, "Now, where were we?"

The steam was gone out of the tirade against me. The group left soon after on cordial terms. That kind of thing never happened again!

God had "set" me, and no individual or group had the power to "upset" me. No matter how bad things seemed, there was an assurance that I was there by God's hand.

Early on, I told the little pastoral staff that unless God showed up in a big way, we couldn't survive. So for the first year, we took turns praying from six in the morning to noon every day. We made it, just barely. But something was starting to thrive. Out of the ashes, a culture of prayer sprouted and took root which would sustain us through all the years.

During these days, Dick Mills, an older prophet whom we had known for many years in California, called me out of the blue. He had a word from the Lord for me: *"I, even I, have spoken; yes, I have called him. I will bring him, and he will succeed in his mission"* (Isaiah 48:15 NIV).

I wasn't afraid of losing my position. In fact, I didn't actually want to be in professional "ministry" and I didn't like being so far from friends and family. But I really didn't know if we would make it. Dick's word gave me hope that the "mission" had a future and that this assignment was more significant than I could have guessed.

INTENTIONALLY CHOOSING FRIENDSHIP

Young leaders often have an internal strength and a radiant conviction toward their particular cause or vision that draws people into the energy-field of that purpose. In Isaiah's words, they come to the *"brightness of your rising"* (Isaiah 60:3 ESV). Strong natural leaders often have a competitive temperament (they like to win) and have an above-average aggressiveness (they are eager to jump into the fray). It's good on a sports field or in a battle against evil, but not so good for reconciling differences.

In Jesus, we've been called to radical re-wiring of our natural inclinations. We are challenged be peacemakers, to serve without selfish interest, and, above all, to love one other. Living in supernatural love is the basis for worldwide transformation! Love seeks to serve rather than to be served, to reconcile rather than to be right. Love pays the price for the mistakes of others. Love comes into negotiations with an unflinching generosity, not a determination to win at the expense of others. Love intentionally chooses to restore broken relationships. It's a very high standard and *way* different from the world around us.

One of the first things we did was to invite Steve, the new senior pastor from our church in California, to come spend some time with us and to preach at the church in Pennsylvania. We were best friends for ten years before the big shake-up. We wanted to close the breach and re-establish good relationships.

I picked him up at the airport and drove him to our little house. Entering through the front door, Steve saw Anne and poured out his heart, "Dear sister, please forgive me. I sat in meetings where people were speculating about you. I knew the truth, but kept silent. I'm so sorry." He was very macho by temperament and so his humility and candor were remarkable.

Anne had a choice to make. This was an opportunity to finally let him know how much devastation had occurred. But like Joseph and full of forgiveness, she responded, "Steve, if you hadn't done that, we would still be in California. What would have happened to all these people? It was God. He meant it for good to help them through this crisis."

Her answer brought a visible wave of relief to our friend and the breach was closed. On Sunday, we introduced him to the people of our church, and I preached on the dangers of offense, with vivid stories of how it had almost killed us and Steve as well.

He preached magnificently that night. The Holy Spirit came in a wonderful way.

When he left, he invited us to come back to visit the church in California and preach the same message I had given in Harrisburg. A few months later we returned for two weeks. It had been almost two years since we drove away in our rental truck.

When the people heard what God had done by sending us to Pennsylvania, how we almost died in our pain, but how He had miraculously placed us in a key place, they laughed and cried. The whole congregation experienced a healing in their hearts. Our friendships were restored. After that, we went back repeatedly to help the leadership team and to preach.

Our extended families were blown away by the restored friendly relations. They would say things like, "We can't believe you would go back after the way they treated you!" We would simply say that we loved them and that it was an honor to help.

Sadly, Steve passed away about fifteen years ago from brain cancer, but when he died we were among his very best friends. He asked us to come back and take the pastorate. What an honor! We couldn't. We were in the middle of a huge property miracle that required us to stay in Harrisburg. But we helped the church through the transition and even found the replacement pastor for them who was then living in Germany. It was a great honor to install him and anoint him and his wife with oil! They've been leading the church for over fourteen years now. This whole episode was a Joseph story. We were happy to help out and demonstrate the love of God in a tangible way and demonstrate the integrity that love always brings.

FRUIT THAT REMAINS

In Pennsylvania, we've been key links in a chain of events that has totally turned the wasteland we first encountered into an open, heavenly paradise! The capital region of Pennsylvania has become a home base for a number of vibrant international ministries that are radically impacting the nations of the earth.[28] It's amazing! Each ministry moved to our city because of a friendship connection with us. These world-changers have altered the spiritual and social climate of our area. Today, the whole region is full of young, joyful missionaries, musicians, and other kinds of love revolutionaries. It is synergistic, with each ministry adding to the others. They are filled with wild hope for the nations, the sort of wild hope that can only come straight from heaven! Anne and I have the awesome honor to be spiritual parents (or grandparents) to a generation that actually believes in worldwide transformation.

We didn't just survive, we have thrived in developing an exceptional team, a creative, joyful spiritual community, and long-term fruitful relationships with significant ministries whose fame and footprint are far larger than our own. Our core team has "done life" together for over twenty-five years! The average age of our faith community was thirty-two the last time we analyzed it. Our Sunday celebrations are full of children, students, young adults, and a few of us older, gray-haired wild ones. The trust level is off the charts! We have been pretty much gossip-free and faction-free for years and years! It's not perfect by any means, but it really is amazing!

LOVE IS THE BASIS OF INTEGRITY

At times we walked through excruciating pain, disappointment, accusation, betrayal, setbacks, and misunderstanding, but through it all we kept our focus on love and kept walking. We discovered that the *Great Commandment* prepares us for the *Great Commission*. Truly the Great Commission will have its

---

28. Some of the key ministries are Global Awakening from St. Louis (2001), Global Celebration from New Orleans (2006), Burn 24/7 from Dallas (2009), and YWAM Fire & Fragrance (2010).

best expression when it flows out of hearts captured by the Great Commandment. Here are a few key principles that will keep you healthy in the midst of the ambitions and pressures of leadership:

Love is the greatest. Whatever you do, don't sacrifice love for the sake of "winning" a dispute, gaining an advantage, or promoting your own fame. This may seem like a no-brainer, but it is harder than almost anything for capable young leaders with forceful personalities. Our voice, our vision, and our energy were designed by our Maker to attract people to us, but it's the day in, day out pursuit of the kingdom of God and its righteousness that will cause your fruit to increase and remain.

What does that look like? The kingdom of God is not a matter of principles or regulations, but of beautiful relationships. It is defined as righteousness, peace, and joy in the Holy Spirit. (See Romans 14:17.) Do you get it? Righteousness, peace, and joy takes us into the divine inner family life of the Trinity! These are royal guidelines for every decision and every relationship. Righteousness, peace, and joy form the practical filter for every decision we make, every plan we lay, every interaction and negotiation we have.

The heaven-sent projects and visions that burn in your heart can only be appropriately expressed in relational integrity, true love shining within your own inner and outer communication. The interaction within your team is the greenhouse for changing the world!

Righteousness, peace, and joy are divine attributes. Let's look at the terms in the Hebrew language that was foundational in Paul's thinking and heart. He wrote in Greek, but his foundation was Hebrew.

Righteousness

Righteousness (the Hebrew word is *tzedaqah*) is all about keeping relationships intact. It is the social culture of heaven. Abraham was in his nineties, but when he looked up at the starry sky and totally trusted that what God had told him was true, all things became possible! He believed that he would have countless descendants. His trust or faith in God's faithfulness made him righteous! (See Genesis 15:6.) At that precise moment, his relationship with God was perfect! He had full access to God's limitless creativity and miraculous ways.

Joseph and Mary were in a crisis. Joseph wrestled in great turmoil with the ludicrous things Mary told him about her pregnancy. She seemed so sincere, but it was so insane. Logically, she must be guilty of adultery, which could result in death by stoning. But, he was a *righteous man,* or as the Jews of New Testament times would say, a *Tzaddik!* (See Matthew 1:18–21.) That is a technical term for a joyful holy man in tune with God. Joseph struggled with how to respond; mercy showed him a way out!

He decided to divorce her. If he gave her a bill of divorce, it would shift the blame from her to him. It would protect her and the unborn child at the expense of his reputation. The divorce certificate would clear her of adultery and put the blame on him as a hardhearted husband! It would even permit her to remarry. And Joseph would look like a total jerk who had gotten Mary pregnant and now wanted nothing to do with her! He would look sinful so she could live.

Do you see? At this point of his sacrificial love, the angel enters into Joseph's dreaming and *blows his mind* telling him about Jesus! Basically, none of us would be saved if Joseph hadn't been truly righteous!

Righteousness makes room for revelation and relationship! It is all about trust and honor. It is *"love your neighbor as yourself"* (Mark 12:31). Love believes the best about others, sees the beauty in others, and sacrifices self for others. It is love's greenhouse in which every person can develop and contribute their greatest potential.

Peace

Peace (the Hebrew word is *shalom*) is understood by scholars to describe the conditions of Eden. Shalom is completeness with nothing missing and nothing broken, just the way it was intended by the Creator. *It is the economic culture of heaven.* It is all that is needed. So I say to you, do not worry about your life, what you will eat or what you will wear, or about tomorrow (see Matthew 6:25, 31, 34, and 10:19), for you are invited into Shalom! And bring all your friends for a preview party of the age to come.

Joy

Joy (the Hebrew word is *simchah*) is the emotional culture of heaven. Everybody's happy! Tears are wiped away. Isaiah foresaw the people of God with their heads (minds) crowned with unending joy! (See Isaiah 35:10.) Sorrow and sighing will flee away; in other words, there will be endless bliss. In His presence is a fullness, an overflow, of joy. (See Psalm 16:11.)

INTEGRITY AND JOY ARE... REALLY IMPORTANT

Now in case you don't think that all this is really the key to leadership and enduring fruitfulness, look again. It starts with the quality of our relationships. That is far more important than the agenda and the projects. Go for love. Love is *the vision.*

Whatever you decide, do, or communicate in your ministry or business, make sure it flows out of love. This is righteousness that releases peace which unleashes joy! Love is the end of the game! It is heaven on earth.

This will have all the nations marveling, "See how they love one another!" Perfect love is the *"revealing of the sons of God"* (Romans 8:19 ESV) that sets creation free!

Integrity is a derivative of *integer*. An integer is a number or an entity that is whole or complete (akin to the Hebrew concept shalom). Love makes us whole and free, and love makes us one.

Jesus prayed that we may be one like the Trinity. It is a plural one, like nothing that's ever been seen! Then the world will believe the Father sent the Son into the world. God's prescription for the cure of every ill is love. In John 13:34 Jesus gives us a new commandment: *"Love one another."* In John 15:10 He calls it *"My commandment."* So simple, but so impossible on our own.

Love is the basis for integrity, for true leadership, for lasting business success, for every life-giving organizational structure. It will cause the nations to sing for joy!

Here's my final appeal for integrity: Make love the matrix for every decision and you will prosper beyond your wildest imagination and have wisdom beyond your years.

CONCLUSION

SEAN FEUCHT AND ANDY BYRD

Forever Marked

On our journey of pursuing integrity, our lives have been forever marked by the stories and testimonies you have just read of the heroes that have faithfully gone before us. What a precedent they have set for us! What a challenge they have extended! The weight of their enormous victories in modeling integrity through all seasons has placed a high standard on all of us following their lead. Through turbulent storms of loss, trials, and temptation, the unshakeable rock of their character and devotion would not move, bend, or change to convenience or relativity. Although they stumbled, the Lord lifted them back up. When they were convicted of sin, they responded by turning back to the Lord. The many tempting lures of the world had no hold on their hearts. They were pledged to obedience in Christ and would not be moved.

> *One generation shall commend your works to another.*
>
> (Psalm 145:4 ESV)

We are living in the confluence of a very dramatic shift of generations across the earth. In virtually all parts of society, the "baby boomer" generation in their sixties and seventies is beginning to pass on the torch of leadership to a new breed. From Wall Street to the White House to the Wednesday night prayer meeting, there are presently (and will soon be more) large vacuums of leadership waiting to be filled. The older generals have boldly and faithfully commended the works, values, and promises of God, and now we must humbly follow. As they stood for truth, justice, and integrity, so must we.

So what do we make of their lifelong testimony and story? There are many more heroes and life-living "billboards" of integrity that were not spoken of or mentioned. If God has done it before, can He not do it again in our generation? By reading these words, we have become responsible for what we now know. We cannot just dismiss this knowledge as momentary inspiration—no, we must be responsible and do something with all we have been given. Inaction is not an option. We must hope, dream, and actually become the manifestation of the cultural reformation! We must become transformed in our character and daily life! All it takes is the pioneering of a few gritty leaders who will not cave in—who will instead stand for truth. Every area of our life is now due for an immense integrity upgrade!

THE LOST GRIT

The pursuit of godly character is truly the "lost grit" in the body of Christ. It is not always marketable or salable. It is rarely seen or even noticed first on the outside. It will never be viewed as sexy and relevant in the sliding moral fabric of our culture. It never comes in a quickly gained, "microwavable" fashion. You cannot respond to an altar call, receive a prayer, and supernaturally possess it. There is a cost and a sacrifice. Integrity is a gut-wrenching, fist-clenching choice. And there is a high threshold to enter into the fullness of its promise. This is why few enter in—few make the choice and engage in a pursuit of it.

Many mock and tout the values and dogma of the heroes before us as "archaic" and "out of touch" with culture. To avoid the appearance of being "exclusive" or viewed as "bigots" in the eyes of culture, many will jeer and steer to stay relevant and tolerant. But by doing this, we cheapen true transformation, grace, and the abundant promises that follow the life of integrity and devotion. The power of the gospel is its *truth* to transform society and turn the world upside down! Do not settle for an inferior or watered-down gospel that caves in to the pressures of society. The gospel always goes against the grain of culture! The fish in the kingdom always swim upstream.

We desperately need to regain the grit of unyielding determination to truth and honesty. Grit is not always pretty, recognized, or vendible, but it is the game changer. Do not buy into the theology polluting the minds and poisoning the hearts of a culture that it is possible to follow Jesus and blend in with the culture. We are *"children of light, children of the day"* as we shine truth, hope, and love (1 Thessalonians 5:5 ESV). You were born as the polarizing force bringing definition to what is right and what is wrong—what is sin and what is truth. Let us rise above the flood of passivity and raise a standard of excellence and obedience to the cause of Christ!

When the enemy comes in like a flood, the Spirit of the Lord will lift up a standard against him.   (Isaiah 59:19)

MAKING INTEGRITY FAMOUS

There's no turning back
No Turning Back
Cause where I'm going
There's no turning back
I put my hand to the plow
I will not look to yesterday
No Turning Back

The words of this song came to me as we handed out our first Bible to an open-hearted group in a very closed nation, years ago. If found out, they could lose their lives for possessing that Book. I will never forget looking into their eyes: they were full of determination, zeal, and the uncompromising grit of certainty that risking their very life was worth the words on the pages of the Book they were receiving.

They were willing to literally lay down their life for a truth they had only just encountered and to die at the hands of an oppressive regime for Christ. There was no turning back. There was no retreat. There was no plan B. There was no "trying it out." We are in such a moment where we cannot turn back from steadfastness of uncompromising character and the truth of the power of the gospel. We must set our hand to the plow of pursuing lifelong integrity and never look again on the past failures, struggles, and sacrifice of all we feel we have left behind.

LOOKING FORWARD

Hopefully the content of this book has stirred your heart to see the beauty and worth of pursuing a life of integrity! We can only imagine the pleasure that it would bring to the heart of Jesus to see His followers reading, discussing, and applying the truths contained in these chapters. The joy contained in living a life of truth in everyday details is too little discussed, too little considered. But that could all change. It starts with a few. It starts with a few zealous, sincere followers who are willing to live differently than the rest. Are you one of those? Are you willing to pay the cost of a life of integrity?

So answer me this:

1. Can you distinguish a life joyfully choosing holiness, purity, and integrity from a life that wears those things like a heavy yoke and attempts obedience out of drudgery?

2. Are you willing to say no to your flesh because you have been struck with the joy of standing before God some day and knowing that you chose Him over momentary pleasures?

3. Are you convicted that your public life is only as powerful as your private life is pure?

4. Are you willing to be misrepresented, misunderstood, and at times judged for making a choice that you know lines up with the character of Jesus?

5. Are you willing to call sin as it is and make no excuses to justify personal pleasure, offense towards others, dishonest communication, or any lack of integrity?

6. Are you willing to be quick to repent when you make a mistake and to live in the light when you fail, instead of sweeping things under the carpet or putting on the garish mask of hypocritical Christianity?

7. Are you willing to walk upstream even if everyone around you drifts down the river of sliding morals, relativistic living, and self-serving lives? Are you willing to

be the last one standing on what is true, right, and full of love?

8. Are you willing to believe that even in the face of extreme darkness that there is always hope? Are you willing to be that hope?

If you can say yes to all the above, then you are ready to bring God tremendous glory! You are ready to represent Him to a world that is desperate for a witness of who Jesus really is! You are ready for a godly marriage that will raise godly children and bring the kingdom through everyday life! You are ready to be a servant leader in the order of our Savior King and heroes of the faith throughout the ages! Let's make history together!

We feel that there are thousands that are ready to say yes to the above questions and dedicate themselves to a life marked with integrity! There are many in this generation who, with smiles on their faces, are ready to pick up their crosses daily and live differently. It is a hero generation like many that have gone before us. However, this generation has not been told that they have a war to fight. Heroes are only made when they have the opportunity to overcome impossible odds. Well, many would say the odds are impossible. Many would say our nations cannot be turned around...but heroes live differently and heroes die with an unflinching hope that their lives of faithful obedience will make a dent in history!

Our desire is that this would not just be another book, but rather that it would be a spark to a growing movement. We desire that this book would catalyze action in individual hearts as well as in a generation. To keep this from being just a good topic and a momentary commitment, we want to direct you to two websites. Check out www.burn24-7.com and www.thecircuitrider.com for updated, transformational content that can be used both individually and in a group setting. Join many others in a commitment to integrity and feed your spirit with ongoing revelation and encouragement to live our lives before the Lord and the world in a way that brings glory to our great God!

To this end, let us labor and live!